WHAT'S THAT IN MY ATTIC?

WHAT'S THAT IN MY ATTIC?

Sean Orford

author of 'The Frog Snogger's Guide' and 'What Colour is Your Knicker Elastic?'

2000

First published in 2002 by Management Books 2000 Ltd
Forge House, Limes Road
Kemble, Cirencester
Gloucestershire, GL7 6AD, UK
Tel: 0044 (0) 1285 771441/2
Fax: 0044 (0) 1285 771055
E-mail: m.b.2000@virgin.net
Web: mb2000.com

Printed and bound in Great Britain by Biddles, Guildford

British Library Cataloguing in Publication Data is available
ISBN 1-85252-402-2

Contents

Dedication

This book is dedicated to Eileen, the Mother I almost had.

Acknowledgments

Sean Orford recognises the contribution made to the understanding of personality archetypes by Christopher Hills and Kevin Kingsland.

Thanks to all clients, students, colleagues and family who encourage me in my work. Special thanks Sue and Debbie for their proof reading and Trish for her work towards the launch of the last book, 'What Colour Is Your Knicker Elastic?' and hopefully the launches of books to come. I must also thank James at Management Books 2000 for his forbearance in the matter of my late delivery of manuscripts.

Introduction

This new book is another steppingstone to self and corporate discovery in the series that has become affectionately known as 'the Frog Snogger's Series' after the first book *'The Frog Snogger's Guide'*. The aim of the series is to enhance the science of communication through the development of our understanding of our relationships both professional and personal. The connection that we make with others is termed 'communication' because this means 'common union or to be at one with'. When we truly communicate, we become at one with the person we are in communication with. It is through understanding and developing our ability to communicate that we are able to resolve the problems and issues that might hinder or prevent our effectiveness and our happiness. The most important of all the relationships that I need to understand is that which I have with myself. This is fully recognised and developed throughout the series. The FSG series is of use to all those needing to understand themselves and others – managers, care workers, therapists, sales personnel, doctors, teachers ... and all human beings.

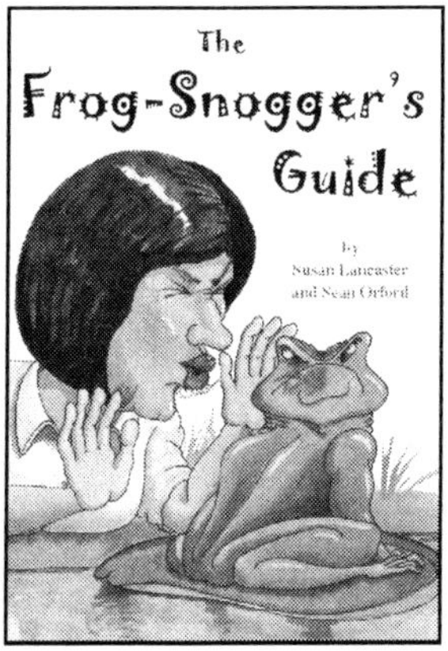

The Frog Snogger's Guide

The first book in the series *'The Frog Snogger's Guide'*, addresses some fundamental problems that exist in many relationships. The book is presented as a guide for dealing with difficult people. The skill of learning to like the unlikeable is developed through the use of a model of personality based on an eastern Ayurvedic psychological system. Each person is identified as consisting of eight primary drives. It is the subtle blending and mixing of these drives that is the basis of the individual personality and our character type. The strengths and weaknesses of these drives create in people the uniqueness that we experience as individuality. It is through knowing how a person's drives are configured that understanding and communication are enhanced and personal effectiveness increased. Included in this is our own development through self-discovery and understanding.

What Colour Is Your Knicker Elastic?

The second book in the series *'What Colour Is Your Knicker Elastic?'* uses the Ayurvedic personality model in developing an understanding of the emotional energies that create, break and maintain our relationships. The natural tendency that we all exhibit to form particular types of relationship is played out in repeated cycles and the re-enactment of past mistakes in current attachments. We have all seen people who leave one partner because of their negative or unacceptable behaviour. When they set up home with a completely different partner they then find that the same problems and issues crop up again. It is as though we are repeating the same problems in our attempt to get beyond them. This principle holds true in both our domestic and business relationships. These relationship cycles are only broken through understanding and knowledge. Sadly such knowledge is usually only gained through experience and pain. Few of us are able to learn from the mistakes of others. Successful relationships only develop when we truly understand our own needs and are able to gauge realistically what it is that the other party is able to offer us.

What's that in my attic?

This, the third book in the series, *'What's That In My attic?'*, examines the hidden, and sometimes darker, side of our unconscious mind. It uses the personality model to explain how past experiences and relationships directly affect our present experience and behaviour. Past, unresolved material that has been stored inside us sometimes referred to as repressions or more commonly as 'baggage', can dictate how we think, feel and act in an every day sense. We are all carrying baggage and some of the bags are heavy and can weigh us down. *'What's That In My Attic'* gives us the opportunity to engage in some major housework as we unpack the unresolved emotions contained in our boxes and bags. As we sweep out the cobwebs from the corners of the cupboards in our unconscious mind we experience a lightening of our load and renewal of hope and personal energy.

Waking Up Is Hard To Do

(Due for publication later in 2003)

The next book in the series, *'Waking Up Is Hard To Do'*, takes us on the next stage in this voyage of self-discovery. Up to this point, we have examined why we are like we are and how past unresolved experience affects our behaviour and our ability to maintain relationships and find personal fulfilment. This new book turns our focus from the past, encouraging us to live in the present and create the future. The process of waking is usually in response to emotional pain. When I hurt, I have little choice other than to change. Changing involves behaving differently. The success or failure of the changes I enact will depend on my degree of awakeness. To be totally awake is to have clear vision. To have clear vision is to be clairvoyant in the sense that I develop an awareness of how my actions will affect me, and those around me. The future is not left to chance – I can become self determining and finally know where I am going.

1

Finding the Way In

Gaining access to the unconscious mind is easy only if you know the combination.

This book is about the boxes and bags of unresolved emotional stuff that we keep hidden deep inside ourselves.

At least it will be once I get going. I am suffering from the blank page syndrome. Well actually it is the blank screen syndrome. I suppose this is what used to be known as writer's block, though I find it is difficult to associate the idea of using a pen to write a passage of prose with that of pressing the keys on the computer keyboard. Perhaps what I am really suffering from would be more correctly described as creative constipation. I am looking for a laxative, something to unblock the creative tubes. You see, for me the process of writing is like attempting to start a rather large and very heavy steam locomotive. It is not easy. It takes such a tremendous amount of energy to get the whole thing moving. There is the whole business of the loading of the water. The stacking of the logs follows this, in something I seem to remember is called the tender. After that, comes the lighting of the fire. Then there is the palaver of getting the whole thing full of steam and up to pressure. It is only at that point that with the wave of a flag, a blow of a whistle, a bang and a hiss of steam that the thing has the brake released and can begin to move off with, hopefully, a jaunty toot. Though, be warned once the monster is on its hissing and creaking way then look out, as the momentum becomes unstoppable.

I need to be left alone now to stoke the boiler. I am out of circulation until the job is done, I don't want to know anybody, just go away and leave me alone.

Thoughts should flow from the mind like wine from a bottle

I am seeking a corkscrew with my left hand while holding a bottle of rather nice Merlot in my left. Maybe my problem is more akin to uncorking a bottle of wine. If only the cork would come out, the wine would flow. I have often read that writers tend to be heavy drinkers, like Dylan Thomas, but then such statements are themselves written by writers. I have never been a stranger to alcohol, something I was introduced to at a very early age. My social training, from the Irish side of the family, heavy drinkers to a man, taught me in no uncertain terms that the etiquette in these matter is that once the cork leaves the bottle it does not go back in. As a child, it was 'bottoms up', and once the bottle was finished there are very often bottoms up literally, and heads down – 'talking to God on the big white telephone' was the phrase I seem to remember. Right now, I am the drinker and I am in need of a corkscrew and I can not find one. I need to allow the juices to flow. For now, it does not matter if it is cork or train, the issue remains the same, how to get it out, how to get started?

It's on the tip of my tongue

Actually I must have started to some extent because I have just written the above and that in its own way begins to address the issues. My dilemma of 'have I, or have I not started' is really the subject of this book. We all have material within us that we may be unable to access. Perhaps it is a word, someone's name of an idea or, that thing that is on the tip of your tongue that cannot be remembered. It matters not a jot how clever are the ideas packed away in bags and boxes in the recesses of our mind – if we cannot get at them, we cannot use them.

If the stuff in the boxes is to be of any use to us at all, we need to be able to get at them when we need to – at will. Yet throughout life, we are continually told in a variety of ways that we should leave it all well alone, that thinking is bad and will bring to no good. We are encouraged not to probe…

'Your problem is that you are too deep…'
'You think too much…'
'Get a life…'
'Stop worrying about it…'

We tend to avoid any self-examination, as it might be painful and involve us facing change. However, we are happy to examine others. It is after all the essence of gossip and all group interaction. In the main, we have a psychosocial pact within our family or group, an unwritten agreement between ourselves not to say or do things that create discomfort to any of those present. The person that is the subject of the gossip is the one who is not there. To face other people with what we feel about them is confrontational, too discomforting, something to be avoided. Avoidance is the game when it comes to looking inside ourselves. Change is destabilising. We avoid change at all costs…

'You made your bed now lie on it…'
'Better the devil you know…'
'Whatever you do, do not look at yourself, change is dangerous and very scary…'

Self discovery can create psychological paralysis

I am not there yet – I remain stuck with the fact that the number one task is identifying the starting point of this book, the starting point of looking within. The unanswered question is how do I get this book off the buffers and make it move. How like a client I sound. Clients come to the first session of psychotherapy and sit looking a bit like a rabbit that has become caught in the headlights of an oncoming car, shaking, nervous and paralysed. The client has come with an issue that deserves resolution and they just do not know where to start…

'I just don't know where to begin…'
'I feel a bit of a fraud now I am here…'
'I am probably wasting your time…'

Alcohol does not take you inside yourself – it sends your brain to sleep

Many clients will use all kinds of excuses to not look within. This makes me wonder about alcohol. When we manage to blank out the problem enough, we can use excuses like those above. That is how most clients begin. They have worked so hard over such a long period to avoid facing the problem, that they have ceased to have an understanding why they are here, what they need to look at or where to start. All they really know is that they hurt and that they would now like it to stop – 'please'. So together we sit and, as if we are in some ritualistic Dervish dance, we begin to circle the problem. In the cupboard in their mind is the bag, box or whatever they have stored their problem in. We need to locate it. We are like a couple of trappers in the snows of the Klondike looking for a rabbit to complete tonight's stew. I know that if we are patient, the animal will break cover and then we will be on it like a pack of ravenous wolves. It is then that our work can commence.

In my writer's mind, I am circling the material of this book now waiting for it to break cover. No – even that is not right. On reflection, I do not feel like a trapper, I am more like a cracksman seeking the combination to a safe. I see myself with a stethoscope held to my temple as I twirl the dial that is my nose back and forth trying to crack the combination. The desperation and frustration can lead me to reach for the enlightening gelignite of fermented grape juice ... there goes another cork, or is anaesthetic? In all honesty, the wine simply seems to slow the process further because it relieves the tension by putting my brain to sleep. That makes me feel better, and when I awake I am faced with the same problem. Where to start?

Letting go is hard to do

This process can go on for days. I don't mean the drinking, I mean the searching. The bottom line is I feel too wound up and need to learn to let go. I feel another metaphor coming on. Constipation is about holding in, holding back. To get rid of it, to empty yourself, you have to let go. You see, I know what I want to write – it is all inside me. If only I could allow myself into that inner place where it is all happening, to where I hold my emotional boxes and bags, I could let it all out whether it is a safe, box, bag or bottle. It has been three days now since I started looking at blank screens. Blank screen-itis.

A mantra is a sound or rhythm that stills the busy mind

These thoughts are running through my head as I drive the motorway from a day clinic in Liverpool, Merseyside to an evening clinic in Mold, North Wales. I am not tooth-tapping as in the first book, (The Frog Snogger's Guide – an absolute must if you haven't already got one), I am steering wheel tapping. It is eternally strange to me how the metronomic effect of tapping stills the mind, well my mind anyway. Steering wheel tapping is not dissimilar to thumb twiddling and finger drumming. One of my hypnotherapy teachers tells the tale of how he managed to induce hypnosis in a woman at a cocktail party by simply tapping his finger on his wine glass in front of her and using a few well-chosen words. A good party trick, though highly unethical – but it makes you think, doesn't it? What power is there in the tap? Makes me wonder about the repetitive beat in pop songs and mass hypnosis? God knows what psychological state tap dancers are in.

My Uncle Sid was a tapper, a steering wheel tapper. Though in his case he had a rather unfortunate tapping style. He tended to tap the underside of the steering wheel in an upward motion in time to whatever Radio Two would throw at him. He said that his tapping put him into a sort of suspended animation in which he was quite unaware of anything until he reached his destination. He would get in the car at one end and apparently a few taps later he had arrived several hundred miles from where he started. The car must have known the way.

I can imagine astronauts on long haul flights to Mars staring fixedly out of the windows whilst tapping the control consul and tapping their way there. In this suspended animation, they would have felt as though they had arrived before they left. Anyway, for Sid, this tapping was all well and good and did help with his travelling until one day whilst in the fast lane of the M4 motorway when he was heading towards London on the wiggly bit that is held up on stilts. As the morning sun streamed through the windshield he was tapping absent mindedly to the Righteous Brother who had just lost 'That Loving Feeling', when his steering wheel parted company with the steering column as 'baby, baby I'll get down on my knees for you' was reaffirmed through the speaker system. Luckily, the Metro, always a dubious choice I thought, stopped in a straight line despite crossing the lanes. The hazard lights worked, which was some sort of blessing and the man from the Royal Automobile Club reattached the steering wheel, which was another, and Sid was on his way. He no longer taps his steering wheel up or down and is known to blanch and run to the bathroom should 'You never close your eyes…' erupt from a speaker.

No red herrings here

This Uncle Sid story is not a red herring; he does have some relevance to this book and the nature of things I hold in my boxes and bags in the cupboard of the inner space within my mind. There is a big box labelled Sid because, when I look at him, I have often questioned whether or not he is actually my father. We look, act and sound so alike and have often been mistaken for each other on the telephone. The fact of my questioning my parentage alone could be the one thing that would, if not excuse, explain my father's treatment of me, I wonder? There are a few more boxes full of stuff on that and associated subjects in my cupboard, which need to be unpacked. These thoughts have over the years worn deep ruts in my mind and currently have a predictable destination. Though relevant to this book, they are not the 'it' for which I am searching – not what I am seeking to start the train of this book in motion. They do not take me to 'the' spot. My mind needs to wander further – 'what is the combination'?

Meditation and relaxation prepare the mind to be receptive

By the time I get to Mold, I have tapped my mind to stillness and I am fairly relaxed though no nearer finding the way into my inner self. In the absolute silence of the empty clinic, I make a mug of black coffee and sit for a while. I like to turn up early to a clinic so that I can arrive mentally and emotionally before the client does and so genuinely be there for the client. I have a little three-minute relaxation/meditation technique, (highly recommended tapes available), that I use to let go of my own thoughts and feelings so that I can begin to focus.

Sitting in the three minutes of still inner space, I am vaguely aware of the answer-phone clicking on, the volume is turned down. When, at the completion of the exercise I open my eye, the little red light on the answer machine is winking at me there is one message. I pressed the buttons with that strangely clear and acute perception and concentration that only comes after meditation. The tape whirrs a rewind, stops and plays forward. The dull, nasal Cockney tones of my youngest sister Karen flow from the speaker (that's Kar as in car – vroom vroom – not Kar as in carrion. Get it wrong at your peril!) 'Ring me as soon as you can – it's urgent'. The message is short terse and to the point. Karen is never a woman of many words unless she is drunk and then you can't shut her up. The apparent dryness of her communication is really only to be expected as any contact between my natal family and myself has been minimal. In fact, I have not met or had any contact with Karen for, I estimate, about six years. It is probably more accurate to say that she has not had any contact with me. I have tried.

Klong is when the innocent face the evidence of their accusers

My first response to the tone of her voice is an emotional rush of klong to the heart. I first came across the word 'klong' in the book *'Presumed Innocent'* by Scott Turow; I think they made a film of the book. In the book, klong is described as the rush of 'shit' or negative energy, to the heart that is felt by the accused when they see the weight of evidence being presented against them. In my consulting rooms, klong is the thing I see flood through clients with a sharp intake of breath when a box in their cupboard is finally open and they realise the enormity of the reality or truth in the issues they are attempting to come to terms with. A good word is klong.

In this case, I am not wrong. The feeling of klong has all the accuracy of clairvoyance. When I find and finally dial my sister's number, she tells me that my mother has had a fatal heart attack and died in the arms of my father that very morning. Despite my sense of shock, I am surprised at how matter of fact Karen now sounds. I guess she must have done a lot of emotional processing between when she first left the message and when I finally got back to her. Either that or she had told the same story so many times it has become like a press briefing. I am speechless for a minute as I rock a little and collect my thoughts. I tell her I need some time to think about this. For me, with my family, there is always a lot to consider. 'I'll get back to you', and I replace the receiver.

It often takes a devastation to open the door to the Attic

As I slump into the chair, I can feel the wheels of the combination lock to the inner safe whizz. As they click to the correct combination, the doors swing open, the train is leaving the station, the wine corks have popped, the constipation is easing, the rabbit has broken cover and is off and away.

Sometimes it takes big events to crack combinations. I have done it and I am in – klong, baggage, boxes and all right at the centre of that place where I store all those things, the feelings, thoughts and images that have remained un-dealt with, my unfinished business. Despite any attempts to keep them closed, the doors of the safe, the cupboard, are bursting open and the emotional contents spills out all over the place. I am buried in an avalanche of memorabilia. Pictures and images of past events chase the feelings around my head and my heart. A process has started.

Over the coming days, weeks and now I discover, months, I recall and remember things that have been buried for many years. The ferocity of the feelings welling up inside me becomes focussed in my throat and seems to be strangling or gagging me. It is here that – from necessity, not choice – I finally let go the constipation as feelings begin to flow. The convulsive power of the abreacted emotion leaves me raw, naked and vulnerable. Bereavement and grief have begun. I know life will never be the same again as I take a step nearer to adulthood. At fifty years of age, I no longer have a mother, I am no longer a mother's son. Whatever hopes and dreams that have always existed in my fantastical potential of what might be could never, will never, now come to pass.

I cancel my clinic.

2

Inner Cupboards

*Discovering the true cause of a problem
is like hunting a rabbit in the Klondike.*

When I first see a client, I invariably set some homework. There are two main reasons for this. From the client's point of view, it allows them to become engaged in the idea and process of therapy. Working on their problem outside of the sessions encourages the development of a positive attitude towards self-discovery and you never know what they can discover. It is not uncommon for the client to return to the second session telling me that in completing the homework, they have seen and solved, or are in the process of solving their problem, and that they do not really need me. If I am not careful, I will put myself out of a job – powerful stuff, homework. The second reason is that it enables me to understand how it is that the person functions internally both emotionally and mentally, what the mechanism is that makes them tick. It tells me a lot about them and tells them a lot about themselves.

Most counsellors are not gurus

In the east, when a student went to a Guru seeking to solve a problem or, at the extreme end, to gain enlightenment, the Guru would require the student to work alongside them for a prolonged period of time. This might have been up to two or three years. The purpose of this was to allow the Guru or teacher to observe how the student behaved and interacted with others so as to gain an understanding of the student's inner world. Observation enabled the Guru to get a feel for what it is the student would need to help them resolve their problems and allow them to learn and grow psychologically and spiritually.

Counsellors and psychotherapists are not Gurus, though some may think that they are. In reality, many counsellors, especially those working in orientations such as cognitive behavioural therapy and rational emotive therapy, tend to use a more directive style, and are sometimes really teachers. Whatever the individual therapist's stance, the counsellor also has a need, as much as the Guru, to understand the inner workings of the client.

Western time scales do not allow for protracted observation. Can you imagine living alongside your counsellor for two years before they started doing any work with you? Other methods need to be employed. Many psychologists use audits, scales and inventories to tell them about their clients. I use a particular type of observation based on the eastern science of Mudra. Mudra is an area of study that employs series of techniques for understanding the inner person by observing how individuals use their bodies and where they exhibit and hold their muscle tensions. Mudra also offers us an understanding of the psychological implications of a particular build, shape, stance and gesture. The use of Mudra is a subject that I address in other books. Apart from using Mudra to observe my clients, I also ask some simple questions related more to my Ayurvedic training. The questions are set as homework. In response to the questions, the client may write a word, a lists or a book.

Setting the homework

So, at the completion of the first session, I ask the client in some form or another to answer the three questions that we have dealt with in the previous books. I do not want an answer there and then. I want them to go away and think deeply about it and write things down that they can bring to the next session. The questions are…

Who are you?

How do you show people you like them or how do you know when people like you?

Where do you place your security?

Remember that in this, the first stage of psychotherapy, the client and I are playing the role of trappers attempting to encourage the rabbit (real problem) to break the cover of the undergrowth (the unconscious mind) and make a dash for it then we can jump on it and sort it out. This may not have happened during this first session and there may be some way to go, some beating of the bushes before the rabbit will run. Often I have seen the rabbit start to run before the client does, but I need to keep my mouth shut. If we are going to be really successful in our work, I need the client to see the rabbit as well. I do not warm to therapies that do things *to* people I like to do things *with* people. This is the point of the homework. My hope is that in the process of working through the three questions, the client will clearly see the rabbit or at least get a feeling for what it looks like or where it is hiding.

Answering the questions

In the second session, we review the client's responses to the three questions. It might be useful to note that clients that are unable or unwilling to answer one or all of the questions are also describing their rabbit as much as those who write a book about them. For example, if I do not know whether or not people like me, I am describing my own lack of social awareness or my state of social isolation. This in turn describes how I live my life and my relationships and will have some bearing on where I do or do not place my security. In general terms, whatever the client's responses are to these questions, they are a description, to some extent, of what the problems is. It then follows on what it is that they will need to do to resolve it and, the resources that they have at their disposal to help solve the problem. Where there is a lack of resources indicated, the answers to the questions will also give some indication as to where the client may go to obtain these resources. From my point of view as the therapist, the answers tell me a lot about what my role will be throughout this therapy and how it is best for us to set about our task. The questions are my version of the Guru's two years' observation.

Setting the trap

The work with the client up to this point will often, in this second session, only have told us how we can deal with the problem. Identifying the rabbit may well be our next task. It will though probably have told us how we should set the trap. We need this to be clear and to understand what it is we are dealing with, what the problems really are. Here the focus must be on the client being able to understand what their problem really is. The reason they came to counselling may be a red herring and we need to identify and acknowledge this. It is not sufficient for the therapist to understand. To reiterate my earlier point, therapeutic change is only effective when it comes from the inside out, from within the client, not the outside in, from within the therapist. When clients work from that point of inner understanding, they retain the power and control over themselves and what happens to them – this include the process of counselling or psychotherapy. It is the business of doing something *with,* not *to* the client. This can be a deep issue that is often fraught with red herrings. It is an issue that is often not understood by therapists. Let me explain.

Psychological red herrings

The reason the client was referred, or has referred him- or herself may not be the real reason they have come even though they may think it is. The likelihood is that they are unaware of this.

> John is a manager. He is thought of highly by his directors and the organisation as a whole. He does, after, all get results. He is the guy

who says 'yes' – the 'can do' manager. His staff hate him. They see him as fixed, authoritarian, and unreasonable. He is a volatile bully. Over a period of six months, four of his staff have come to see me, through self-referral, for counselling in the occupational health department, for being bullied by John. None of the four feel they could stand up to the rigours of the disciplinary process within the organisation. They are aware of how popular John is with higher management and suspect that after whatever process of complaint was enacted, they would be in a worse position and that John's behaviour towards them would become more vicious. John managed a team of twenty-eight people. I listen to the stories of bullying over the months from these four employees. When I review my caseload, I note that these four clients have some things in common with one another...

- All were female.

- All reported, at some point during the counselling that they had been abused as children, two sexually, one physically and one mentally.

- These issues had never been attended to or resolved and had in each case been denied by the mother when mentioned by the client.

- In each case, the abuser was male, one father and three stepfathers.

- The abuse had taken place behind closed doors and, in each case, the client had been too scared to discuss what was happening with anyone else beyond their efforts to gain the support of their mothers. In the physical abuse case, a teacher had realised what was happening and attempted to have something down about the situation. This was seen as making the problem worse and nothing ever happened or was proved. In short it was swept under the carpet by the social workers involved.

- In all four cases, the abusive acts only ceased when the client left home. They all left home at an early age.

- All four had made attachments to men who were older than them. Each partner had carried on the abuse in the style of original perpetrator.

- None of these staff felt able to stand up to the manager or the organisation. All four resolved this problem by leaving and finding work elsewhere.

In reviewing these fours clients, it becomes clear to me that the reason they came to see me was not because of the manager John. It was really because they had unresolved issues of abuse. These issues had/were being held deep inside them and had never been dealt with. I am not suggesting that John is not a bully I have many other examples that would show clearly that he is.

As far as I can ascertain, the treatment metered out to these four was no different from that of other staff in the group. No other staff came forward for counselling or reported problems when given the opportunity. All indications are that the four were reacting to being victims of abuse at an earlier stage in their lives. Their problem was mainly this earlier abuse, not John's behaviour.

I am not suggesting that John's behaviour is acceptable – it is not. The important thing is that past experience and unresolved emotion colour and affect our present experience and behaviour. These four clients, just like the rest of us, are holding unresolved negative emotional experiences deep inside in the dark recesses of the unconscious mind. As a footnote to these clients, three of the four chose to go on to sort out the past abuse issues, one with me and two with specialist services. The remaining one is, as far as I know, still carrying the heavy and painful bags of her abuse around with her and maintaining her negative self-image as a victim.

Negative energy can even be held in our muscle tension

In most cases, when someone visits a psychotherapist, general practitioner or alternative therapist, the presenting issue is not at the centre of the problem. Many touch therapists will tell stories of when they were working on a client's neck. Suddenly in the middle of a session the client not only relaxed but as the tension came away from her muscles she burst into tears and talked about the loss of her mother, her impending divorce, the imprisonment of her wayward son or whatever.

Julie had referred herself to an aromatherapist because she felt her body was stiff and tense and at times even painful. The tension in her neck meant that she was having problems looking behind her over her shoulder when she was driving. Recently she had a near miss when she failed to see another vehicle coming alongside as she went to overtake the car in front. This had scared her.

The aromatherapist was using massage techniques to work on Julie's spine with an emphasis on her neck and shoulders. After the second session, Julie found that her sleep pattern was disturbed by several dreams. These dreams, almost nightmares, all focussed around the death of her mother three years previously. The tension in her neck had been growing since the death but Julie had not made the connection between the tension and the loss. Actually, the unresolved grief from the loss of her mother had been stored in the muscle tension in her shoulders and neck. At the time of the death, Julie was the one who had found her mother after a heart attack on the floor of the bathroom. She had attempted mouth-to-mouth resuscitation until the ambulance men arrived. Her mother was pronounced dead on arrival at the hospital.

As the eldest daughter Julie experienced the need to keep the family together. Her father, brother and sisters could not cope and happily went to pieces in the knowledge that Julie would come up trumps and do what needed to be done. Julie also believed that she should do this because that was her role in life and had been the way she had always acted in the family. She arranged the funeral and the bun fight afterwards. After the funeral, her father began to treat her as a surrogate wife and expected Julie to look after him with food, washing and ironing, housework and shopping just as her mother had done. Julie had no time to deal with her own feelings. They were stored away in her muscle tissues and were only released, years after the event, in the aromatherapy session. Julie's decision to attend for therapy describes the fact that, for the first time, she gave herself time. Her conscious understanding or her unconscious tension led her to change her life. Even massage can be psychotherapeutic.

In this case, the muscle tension is only the symptom, the cause is the trapped grief that has not been processed. Many of my clients have unprocessed emotions that have been stored in their unconscious mind and on occasions also in their muscles. These tensions that are reflected in the body are the subject of the science of Mudra (see above). When I walk my client from the waiting room to the consulting room, I am observing to make the connections between the mind and the body, the spirit and the body, the psychology and the body or, whatever term you would use to describe the inner self. Both the inner state and the outer state of the physical body are a reflection of each other. They both affect each other. Therapies on one of these will directly and immediately affect the other, so that working on the body muscle tensions can lead to the release of repressed emotional and psychological problems. Likewise, working on psychological tensions will release the repressed tensions held in the muscles.

- **Clearing the mind reduces body tensions.**
- **Relaxing the body reduces psychological tension.**

The magic of practices such as Tai Chi, when taught by an experienced teacher, is that both psychological and physical tension can be attended to at the same time. This all takes us back to the issue of storage and the place deep inside us where we keep or hide our unresolved emotional stuff.

The cupboard in the mind

The client may come to see me because they are having problems with a disturbed sleep pattern due to vivid and scary nightmares.

When this occurs, the sufferer will normally be discharged from sleep in the early hours of the morning in a state of panic. It is only when we work with the contents of the dreams that the real reasons and problems become clear. Both nightmares and disturbing dreams are the symptoms of emotional and psychological tensions stored in the unconscious mind.

Julie's emotional tensions were stored in the muscles of her shoulders, but there would also have been a corresponding emotional and psychological tension. For the therapist, there remains the problem of identifying the actual problems or issues rather than the presenting one. The quickest way to determine the reality of the presenting and the actual problem is to ask what it is the client is keeping in their inner cupboard or attic. This might happen during sessions two or three. The therapeutic bond is developing between the client and myself so that the client no longer appears as apprehensive. They have become involved in their own therapeutic process. It is then that I first begin to describe the cupboard.

> 'Here'...and I point, (you need to point, drawing a two-foot square to the left of my head) '...is a cupboard, we all have one,' I say. 'It's like one of those hall cupboards, you know, one with double doors, like in those old black and white Hollywood movies. The hall cupboard that, if you dare to open it, all the contents will spill out all over your head and bury you, cricket bats, balls, boots and shoes, jumpers, coats and that old lamp that Auntie Bertha gave you for Christmas ten years ago...the one you stuffed at the back of cupboard because you couldn't stand it.'
>
> When they are nodding and I know they are on board with the image, I say, 'I want to know what is in your cupboard. An inventory must be made. In the cupboard, there are boxes that have labels like pain, hurt, loss, grief and bereavement. They may have the names of people or events, lost dreams and hopes.' I ask them to have a good look in their cupboard and begin to list some of the major boxes. 'This' I say '...will tell us what it is we need to deal with'.

This exercise is given as homework – powerful stuff, homework. As with the three questions, the client may find and resolve their issue through this exercise alone. Discovering the contents of a cupboard will often take some reflection and consideration. Some people will be working on material that is recent, fairly near the front of the cupboard. Others will be working at the back of the cupboard and need to revisit places and events far back in childhood.

In some, we will identify one box that demands attention. The process of therapy may be short as we nip into the cupboard, sort out a box and leave the remainder just as we found it. As the Americans say: 'if it ain't broke, don't fix it.'

For many people, the boxes are connected, sometimes the connections follow a tortuous route and dealing with one box reveals problems in others. In these cases, the process of psychotherapy becomes a form of inner housework in which the client is required to clean out the cupboard. It is in so doing that they are able to process the unprocessed emotions within themselves and finish unfinished business.

Some of the contents will be easily and quickly processed and can simply be consigned to the bin. Some will no longer be recognised and be redundant and out of date and no longer needed. This can be taken to the charity shop or recycled. Many of the boxes will contain live material. It may be many years old but it remains live and well, just waiting or demanding to be attended to. These boxes will need to be unpacked and the contents resolved.

Psychological housework in one form or another is to some extent the process of all forms of psychotherapy. The products of the therapy are the issues that are resolved after we have completed the process and our change of mood, attitude, relationships and behaviour.

Once we have sorted the boxes, there may be some that we choose to keep. These can be put back neatly in our spring-cleaned cupboard so that the doors of the cupboard can easily be shut and remain comfortably closed. When the doors can close easily without the intervention of displacement activity – drugs, alcohol or any artificial means – we are starting to reach our own unique version of what we would call 'normality'. It is then and only then that we can begin to feel relaxed, calm and back in one piece, truly whole. Then the therapy is successfully completed.

Collective images in the unconscious mind

Every box, bag and cupboard that we create to store our unresolved emotions exists within us. Our self-concept, our image of who and what we are, exists partly as a result of the types of boxes that we have stored. This is the energy that is described as being 'within us yet beyond our control' and plays a major part in how we feel about our self and whether we like our self or not. The way in which we see ourselves will dictate how we interact with the world.

Simplistically, some people are confident whilst others remain shy, some active and some passive, some loud and some quiet, some thinkers and some feelers and so on. However we manifest our self-image, it does give us an understanding of who we are, our status, position and how we fit into the world at large.

Images are powerful things. People such as Freud and Jung believed there are shared images that float in the collective unconscious of the human mind, a sort of collective unconscious cupboard that we all share. These are images that we share regardless of race, gender, age or colour. A lion is commonly used as a symbol of power and majesty, the mouse is not. The snake or serpent takes on the role of evil that crawls on its belly, the white dove does not. The dear sweet pussy is forever a cuddly 'little pussykins' unless you are the poor mouse that it is batting playfully around the garden.

Just last year, the team of counsellors that I run had a Christmas meal together, one of our how-we-stay-together meetings. The chef, an arty-farty type, had presented the food with his usual artistic flair. The turkey parcels were set amidst a gravy coloured coulis in the centre of a rather large plate, to one side of which were two roast potatoes. This would have been all right if the chipolata with the bacon wrap had not been placed between the potatoes, every bit a set of male genitalia. Mr Freud was having a field day. This was after all a therapist's convention – phallic or what? As a final encore a sprig of parsley had been set at the top of the sausage as an artistically placed garnish, precisely like well-groomed green pubic hair. You can probably imagine the response of the gathered throng, each having their individual particular theories as to the real significance of the placing of the artefacts. I can confirm that this was not a deliberate act as the poor man nearly died of embarrassment when we pointed this out. This was the unconscious manifestation of the chef. He was expressing himself. We all do it all the time. We share archetypal images at an unconscious level. I have run many groups and courses on dreams and Gestalt approaches to repetitive images presented to us by our unconscious mind. One of the most powerful of these images common to all of us is the use of an imaginary house as an expression of our self-concept. Houses and our place in them or connection to them often appear as part a dream story or theme. Understanding your unconscious house is a large aspect of understanding yourself.

Discovering your unconscious house

There is a rather useful exercise used in both Gestalt 'figure and ground' exercises and visualisation or self-discovery exercises. It involves the use of your imagination to decide what your inner house is like. Try this exercise before we move on. Bear with the whims of an old man for a minute and complete the exercise below and then we will return to the psychotherapeutic meaning of what your house signifies. This is a visualisation exercise and will feel more comfortable to those undertaking regular meditation or relaxation session, and if you do not you should.

> Sit quietly alone, preferably in a darkened room. You might choose to play a little music to help you relax. In your mind's eye, picture a house. Do not attempt to force your mind to create or reject a particular house – simply allow the image to create itself in your mind. Once you begin to firm up an image, take a good look around it. Check the outside and if you are able to, have a good look inside. Check out the rooms – how many there are and the different uses to which they are put. Enjoy having a good nose around. Take as long as you like and if you need to revisit your house, you can at any time to check any details you might have missed.

If you have not used visualisation techniques before, you may find that your mind has a tendency to wander off task. This is normal though the more you relax or meditate, the greater is your power to concentrate in all aspects of your life. When attempting the exercise above, if your mind wanders, do not get angry or frustrated. Observe where your mind has gone, let that thought go, do not fight it – just let that thought drift away and return to the task. If you would like to learn to meditate, email me.

Having completed the exercise, sit with your eyes open for a minute as you allow your conscious mind to capture the image of your house. Use the space below to capture the image.

Your House

Ask yourself the following questions.

Is your house set in a garden?

If yes what is it like... formal, scruffy etc.

How old is your house?

What state of repair is it in?

How large is your house?

How many floors does it have?

How many rooms does it have?

What are they used for?

Do you have an attic?

Would you be able to visit your attic?

Do you have a cellar?

Would you be able to visit your cellar?

The theory of Gestalt figure and ground suggests that we can only recognise something outside our self because we also recognise it within our self. So, I can only know that you are an insensitive, unreasonable pig because I also have those qualities within myself to refer to in order to understand you. If I did not have those reference points within me, I could not see them referred in you. Equally to see you as clever, honest, sexy, amazing, wonderful, and so on means that I must have those inner reference points inside me in order to see them in you.

It is important to note that although I might have these qualities of brilliance and cleverness within me, I may deny them and allow them to lie dormant. If I see something in someone else, it is also within me. If I see it out there, it is also in here too. Because of this natural psychological mechanism, the way in which we experience the world is really, and only can be, self-descriptive. As such, we all have a biased view of what we perceive. The common example of this is the one of whether or not we see the glass as half full or half empty. In all our experience, unless we know our self very well indeed, we project our bias and our expectations onto events, objects and people.

In this exercise, I have asked you to imagine a house. I could have asked you to imagine a tree, a car, a cake, a bag of spanners – anything. However you described your house is an expression of how you see yourself. Had it been cars, you may have described yourself as a fast sports car, a luxurious limo, a people carrier or an old banger. For us, houses will do. We are looking predominantly at houses and gardens – sounds like a magazine. Remember your description is a description of how *you* see *you*. Your answers to the questions above described how you see yourself in the world and social setting, including the primary relationship that you live in. If you read and begin to understand your answers, you will start to see what you need to do to bring about appropriate change in your life.

Is your house set in a garden?

The space around your house is the environment in which you live. It may be formal or more native. What you are describing in your image is the way that you feel about the world you experience yourself to be in, the atmosphere of the world that surrounds you. This is your social or family space. It may be rich and warm or bleak and barren. Compare your description of the space around your house to the world you live in. Does one reflect the other?

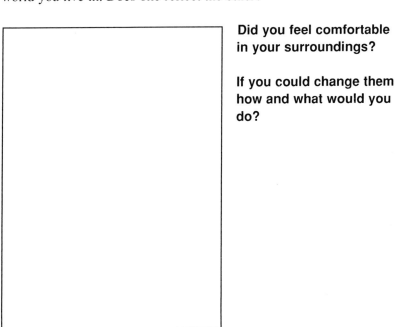

Did you feel comfortable in your surroundings?

If you could change them how and what would you do?

You might choose to review your social life and maybe improve it.

How old is your house?

This description is about how you see yourself not in chronological age more from the point of maturity and style. There are images that we individually associate with Victorian, Edwardian, Georgian etc buildings.

Whatever your chronological age, how old do you actually feel?

Is your age important to what might you want to do or wish you had done?

What age would you like to be seen as?

Issues of aging are often subjects raised in therapy. Psychotherapy is a powerful means of coming to terms with your aging.

What state of repair is it in?

This description is about your ability to attend to your needs. It may be that your description is of a weather-beaten house with peeling paintwork, placed under a sunny sky that makes you feel warm and comfortable – that for you is a good and positive self-description. It may be that your house is in a state of disrepair because it has been neglected. This would suggest that it is you that has been neglected either by yourself or unappreciated by an unloving or over-bearing partner or other significant figure.

Are you well kept and tended, loved and cared for?

Or do you need some attention?

Do you need a make-over or simply some tender loving care?

Does anyone take care of you?

What repair work would you carry out on yourself?

States of repair often relate to levels of fitness, weight, clothing, hairstyles and so on. Getting fit and staying fit is a powerful aspect of our self-image.

How solid is your house?

This description is of your sense of status and solidity. The bigger the building the more difficult it can be to keep it tidy and organised. The more and varied the space the more varied aspect there are of you. Remember the description is a description of you.

Is your mind a great big rambling structure?

Is it more compact and well organised?

Are you an imposing edifice or a squat pile?

How many rooms on how many floors do you have?

Does what was inside match the outside?

Are you an impressive façade with little behind?

Are you a secret Tardis hidden behind a modest frontage?

What would you need to make you a more solid/stable person?

Solidity relates directly to security. When we feel safe and secure, we feel our own power. Developing a solid house involves understanding and developing our own security base.

What are the rooms used for?

Rooms in houses have purpose. Some are everyday relaxed spaces others formal stiff spaces. Some houses are a space in which the owner can hide so that the front door is there to keep people out. Other houses are the centre of a social hub where the door is never locked.

What use is your house put to?

Is it a place that others could easily visit?

Is it a secret private domain?

Is your house for the use of a family or a business?

What rooms would you like to add to your house?

We all have many facets – however we rarely discover them all. Some people feel that they could do almost anything, others that they can do very little. Adding rooms to your house is like developing skills and discovering parts of yourself previously hidden. Time to build an extension.

Does your house have an attic?

When the attic of an inner house is easily accessible, people are able to use their imagination to solve problems. They are able to go to the heights up into the light and let themselves go. People who are unable to go to their attic or are unable to create a house that does have one are usually those who find change and new ideas difficult. They tend to be those that do not like to think too deeply and will often seek to avoid change, wanting things to stay as they are and always have been.

Do you have an attic?

Is it easily accessible?

Are there windows to let light in?

Is there a good sized space under the rafters or do you need to crawl on your hands and knees to enter?

Would you like to enter and understand your attic?

Understanding the contents of your attic comes from taking the time to understand yourself. This is not a highfalutin process. It comes from asking the question: why? Why do I feel, think and act the way I do? Why do I eat what I eat, visit where I visit and so on – simple questions.

Does your house have a cellar?

When the cellar of an inner house is easily accessible, people are not afraid to go inside themselves and face difficult issues. The dark side of the unconscious can be very scary; it is the stuff that nightmares are made from. When the cellar is not accessible or does not exist within the image of the house, the person is either unable or unwilling to face, or face up to, difficult or dark issues within themselves.

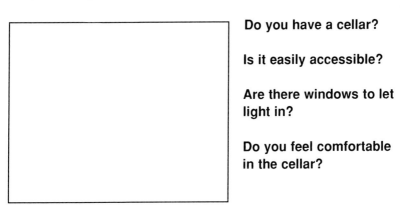

Do you have a cellar?

Is it easily accessible?

Are there windows to let light in?

Do you feel comfortable in the cellar?

The contents of cellars are the subjects of therapy. They are the places that we use to store our negative and darker experiences, the things that we find it difficult to deal with. Cellars are scary and full of things that we have avoided – they are therefore, by definition, difficult to access. Therapy teaches us that, once we are prepared, it is safe to enter the cellar. Our increased understanding equips us with the tools we need to dare to enter the dark. In therapy, we enter the dark in the knowledge that we will not become damaged by the experience.

The responses to the descriptions above should begin to tell us something of what is happening in our unconscious mind. All these images are flavours that, through our descriptions, tell us how we see our self and the world that we live in. All descriptions are individual and therefore unique to the experiencer, though there are particular types of house or archetypes that exist within our imaginations as part of the collective unconscious.

The house archetypes come in eight major varieties. They are really descriptions of the eight major personality archetypes in the Ayurvedic personality model that we have begun to examine in the previous books. I have also included the polar opposites of black and white. White is the wholeness of light before it becomes split into the spectrum of colour. White is often seen as the state of enlightenment or pure love, as in the white dove of piece. Black is seen as altogether negative as the state when all the colours of a paint palette are mixed together. in a state of darkness related to states of despair and hatred.

The Red Physical Self Image

Solid Isolated House

The person who sees them self as predominantly physical will describe an inner house that is solid and strong. Often set alone in an informal setting or garden that may be wild and totally left to nature. The house is often basic and functional. This is not a house designed for pleasure it is for shelter. In some cases it may only be considered as a place to sleep and eat in. It may appear as a cave or simply a strong solid hut or log cabin.

The Orange Social Self Image

Friendly Welcoming House

The social house is altogether a different experience to the physical one. This house is usually fashionable and set in place with other similar houses. Often situated on an estate of similar, if not identical, houses. The gardens are well kept and there may not be fences separating front gardens. The whole neighbourhood may be neat and tidy but will have the sense of being homely and lived in. The social house is more sensual than the functional physical house. Carpets, curtains and floor coverings will have a textural component that is stroked by the owners. Cuddling a cushion whilst watching the television may be comforting. The colours will reflect the trends of the day, will probably be bright and the house will have the openness of the 'knocked through' lounge and dining room. It will be comfortable. The garden is often an extension of the house – the garden room – a place for children to play, swings, slides and paddling pools.

The Yellow Experiential Self Image

Novel Different House

This is probably a strange, impractical and sometimes daft house. It has all the weird and novel features not found in other types of houses. Often it will be composed of energy conserving devices developed from rearranged scraps gleaned from skips and rubbish piles. There is often a strong emphasis on recycling. Unlike the social house where furniture is soft sensual and comfortable, the experiential house is filled with furniture because of how it looks not how it functions or feels. The chair you are sitting on may have been constructed from reclaimed driftwood. If it is comfortable, that is a bonus. This is a house in which we see the rearrangement of the everyday objects into novel and new forms. We are encouraged to see the world from a different angle. The beer can with its top removed has become a flowerpot. Bricks and reclaimed timbers have become bookshelves. The experiential house may be a tent, wigwam, a gypsy's hooped caravan, or a hand-built, jungle night shelter. Whatever it is, it will be different. Gardens may be untidy and carry on the theme of 'alternative' life styles, providing organic food and strange ranges of unknown vegetables.

The Green Egotistical Self Image
'Look At Me' House

This is the... 'Look at me – aren't I rich and famous' house. Ostentatiousness is everything. All of this house shouts or evens screams just how wonderfully successful we are and we want to demonstrate it to you. This house wants to stand out from the crowd. It is the house with huge, out-of-proportion double gates with an automatic opening device operated from the dashboard of the 'look at me aren't I wonderful' car. It is fenced with black railings with spikes and points in gold. The need to be seen with special recognition can drive some people to clad their terraced house with highly inappropriate decorative blocks or turn an ordinary everyday house into a mock Tudor mansion, medieval fortress or a Norman castle. The garden is full of the flashiest barbeques, canopies, gazebos and lighting. Floral planning will be loud and may border on the outrageous. In all the opulence and the price tag is overt.

The Blue Logical Self Image
Sensible Organised House

This house may actually be the same model as the egotistical one above – it is just that it does not need the flashy attachments. This house is designed to express status, safety and security. This truly embodies the sense that 'the Englishman's home is his castle'. It is solid, organised and methodical. It is clean neat tidy and ordered, with a place for everything and, everything in its place. When the best of things are purchased, it is because you only get what you pay for. When you buy good quality goods, they are made to last. The garden is likely to be methodical and ordered to the point of being manicured. Hedges have perfectly straight edges and everywhere there are defined lines. Lawns are edged, bushes are pruned – it is tidy and clean.

The Indigo Intuitive Self Image

Sensitive Harmonious House

This house may come in many sizes. In all Indigo houses, the atmosphere will be aesthetically pleasing. The décor will reflect a modest comfort both within and without. Items used in the home will be chosen with care so that they compliment all that surrounds them. I think it was William Morris who said we should only have things in our houses that are either beautiful or useful. Colour schemes in these houses are sensitive, often embracing the dark blues, lilacs, violets and purples. This house has a serene stillness that is so profound it can be heard. A place of love and sensitivity where to be in a state of tranquillity, peacefulness and relaxation is the natural order of things. The natural stillness and peace of the garden will reflect the serenity and tranquillity of the house.

The Violet Creative Self Image

Innovative House

The creative house is up for grabs. Creative people will create their self-image and recreate it at will. As they do their house may change. Essentially it is either a place in which to create, as in studio, workshop and so on, or the product of the creative process as in innovative design and the positive application of groundbreaking technology. At the extreme the house designed as a place in which to be creative may be a garret and totally basic. At the other end the creatively created house may look unlike anything we would recognise as a house. The gardens will reflect the creativity of the house.

The Magenta Fantastical Self Image

Sugar Plum House

This is the sugar loaf house from Hansel and Gretel. It is Roger Rabbit and loony toons. It is a fantasy that may in reality be impossible, yet in the fantasy it exists and functions. Like some weird place in a dream where all the laws of nature and physics are suspended where the impossible becomes possible as long as it is never put to the test of reality. The house in the fantasy may appear apparently normal yet that house set in reality becomes unobtainable. That is the fantasy and the reason the fantasy exists. The fantasy is an alternative to an unacceptable reality. Fantasy homes are generally very safe, warm places. However, fantasies can be negative and if the person is plagued with negative or repressed emotional material, then it can become very scary, just like a nightmare, and indicate psychological disturbance that may require psychiatric help.

The Black Meaningless Self Image

The house of despair

When life ceases to have meaning either because of inner hurt, despair or what would commonly be termed madness, the inner house is a very dark place indeed and may in the extreme cease to exist altogether. At this point the person may be near to suicide. There is no outside, no surrounding environment. The person has withdrawn into himself or herself only to find that all within is negative black and meaningless. They have gone to an internal hell where medication might be the only thing that is capable of holding it back, though medication does not always have a positive effect.

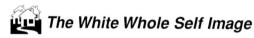

The White Whole Self Image

The house of love

All of the houses described above belong to those that have some form of attachment. The red house is attached to the physical body and physical gratification, the orange house to social networks and sensual gratification and so on. Even the black house has an attachment to the negative. The white house, if that does not sound too presidential, is a place beyond colour and yet it has all the colours within it. Just as your description will probably have aspects of some or all of those above, the white house is the perfect balance of all colours. The white house is the perfect place of rest and ***being*** as opposed to ***doing***.

It is the house of healing and love, the ashram, the hospital (in the broadest sense), the spiritual dwelling.

❍ **All images exist in our unconscious mind.**

The unconscious mind

Our unconscious mind exists below our awareness. Unless we are really awake to what is happening around us, we can only glimpse the unconscious and its effects at odd times. An exercise such as the one we have just done allows us just such a glimpse. Check the description of your inner house. What sort of house is it? The houses as described above are archetypes and your house may have elements from more than one of these descriptions and you may feel that it falls between two or three of the descriptions. This is because there are different parts of your self that are active in your personality. From the previous books, you will understand that our whole being is a construction of eight primary drives. It is the subtle mix of these drives or colours that creates our sense of individuality, my sense of me, your sense of you.

Some people have a very clear image of their inner house. This describes a very strong edge to the personality who is self-aware. These personalities have a very clear image of themselves in an everyday sense. Whatever your description of your house, it is primarily a description of you and how you see yourself. The roots of our self-image as reflected in the image of the house are buried deep in our unconscious mind. By definition, the unconscious is not directly available to conscious self. It is rather like light in that light cannot actually be seen. We can only see what light illuminates. Even the beam of a searchlight seen in the night sky does not show the light itself. What we are seeing are the particles of dust, dirt and pollution suspended in the air that are picked up and illuminated by the beam of light. In the same way we are unable to see the unconscious. What we are able to see are the effects of the unconscious mind as it manifests itself, or reflects itself, in our everyday attitudes and behaviours.

Trapped emotions are repressions

Freud believed – and I think he had a point – that emotional material trapped within the unconscious mind determines how we think feel and behave. These trapped emotions he termed 'repressions'. In his therapeutic experience, he discovered that when working on a repressed problem it would only resolve itself when the emotions trapped in the unconscious mind became conscious. It is only when we can see and understand why we think, feel or act the way we do that we can change it. What he was describing is that the unconscious repression is the cause of a conscious act such as a phobia. The conscious act is the symptom of that cause and the symptom will go away or be altered when the cause or repression is released, changed or altered.

Psychotherapy is a process of waking up

The western psychotherapeutic process of bringing the unconscious repressions to conscious understanding is similar to the eastern process of waking up or increasing consciousness. In a Freudian sense, it is when the unconscious cause of the problem becomes conscious that the problem is solved. In an eastern or Ayurvedic sense, when all that is unconscious has become conscious the individual becomes enlightened. To use the previous image, they become full of light. Here we are beginning to stray into the next book in this series so I will rush back to the plot of this one.

Other people in the house

Most people when using their imagination to visit their inner house within their unconscious mind will be alone in their image. There will be no one else or no other living thing included in the image. This is because the house that we imagine is solely a description of our self and does not include the images of other beings.

When the image starts to include animals and other people, the image is describing to what extent those other beings have become included in the person's own self-image. We often say that dog owners will grow to resemble their dogs. In reality, the supposed similarity is as a result of the tuning in between the dog and the owner. The dog owner is including the dog into his or her self-concept and subsequently will allow the dog to reside in their inner house. Sadly we are unable to know what it is that resides in the dog's inner house or kennel.

In relationships, it is possible – though not very common – to become so close to a partner that they also reside in the inner house. When this happens, we will often see one partner follow the other at the point of death. When one partner dies, the remaining partner has lost half of his or her self-image so they have in fact partly died. The same may be true for someone who has lived through their job role. Thus, single teachers who have nothing other than work in their lives may include children and other aspects of their working life in their inner house. At the point of retirement, an aspect of the teacher dies and in so doing he or she loses the will to carry on living. The same may be true for a dog when their owner dies. I am told that swans mate for life and they will pine to their death after the loss of their mate. They, person, swan or dog, may simply be feeling the affects of the loss of their other half. Without it they simply fade away and die.

There is often a negative association to people that inhabit our unconscious house. Most other people that do appear in our inner house are not there by invitation. They have made forced entry usually through the vehicles of violence or fear. When doing internal housework with clients, I have found that others in the house have appeared after burglaries, assaults, road traffic accidents, trauma that has led to post-traumatic stress disorder, hostage situations, torture, rape and abuse. In short anything that takes total control away from an individual so that they are in the power of another person.

The symbols of rape

In his analytical hypnotherapy course, Neil French includes the story of a female client who was plagued with a repetitive dream. In the analytical world, most practitioners accept the use of the archetypal image of a house as a description of our self in both dreams, fantasies and in exercises such as the one above.

> In this dream the client reports being in a large and well-appointed house. Upstairs there is someone moving about. She knows spontaneously that this is a man and a source of threat. She finds herself searching through the house in a state of anxiety and fear needing somewhere to hide, at the same time knowing that the man will find her. At the bottom of the stairs, she comes upon a dead white cat. The animal has had its belly slit open with a knife. The white fur is stained with blood from the wound. The client knows instinctively that the man did it. The man is coming to get her. The client awakes from the dream in a state of distress.

This is a useful example because it begins to tell us something about how symbols are used by the unconscious mind through the medium of the dream. The contents and story line of the dream, and in this case it is repetitive, is the unconscious mind attempting to process the unresolved repressed material being held by the client in her internal cupboard. To read the dream at a basic level would be something like this; the house is a description of the woman herself just as your description of your house is a description of you. The man upstairs, who is in the bedroom, is the man who raped her. The fact that he is in the bedroom is a symbol in itself and represents her intimate spaces that have been invaded, not just genital but emotional and deeply personal and private. It is useful to note that when clients are in the depth of depression, they will withdraw back to their bed as the ultimate safe space where they cannot be harmed. The bed and the bedroom will for most people have that image of private intimacy. The white cat, or pussy, at the foot of the stairs is where we have a clear genital, and possibly virginal, connection. There is also a connection here between the placing of the cat at the base of the stairs, which is the only route to and from her intimate spaces, and the man being upstairs in the bedroom. The cat has been violated with a knife. The knife is accepted as a phallic symbol representing the man who in this case is a dangerous one. The pure whiteness of the fur – virginity or purity – is stained and defiled as a result of the knife or phallus penetrating the pussy. The cat is ripped open. It is dead. We must assume that an emotional or psychological part of the woman has also undergone an inner death as a result of the sexual assault. In this example, the images and symbols used by the woman's unconscious mind are fairly universal and relatively easily interpreted. In other cases, images and symbols may be more complex and would require some knowledge of the mental frameworks in which the person lives, including cultural norms, to understand their true significance to the dream and the individual.

Reinterpreting the interpretation

In the example used above, there are images. However these relate to the woman as a victim of the rape, they are her conscious interpretation of her unconscious repressions about the trauma she has suffered. In reading her description, you, in your turn, have reinterpreted the images to fit your internal unconscious framework. If you review her description and revisit the images that it evoked in your imagination as you read it, you will be seeing another description of yourself. All the images that I have of the house, the woman, the man upstairs and the cat etc., will be different from yours because my images will be self descriptive of me as yours will be self descriptive of you. In your interpretation, the house you imagined is in some way a description of you and how you see you. This is a huge issue. If you fully open yourself to it you will instantly change your experience of your entire life. If you are able to make this realisation, it will help you begin to understand the true relationship that you have to people, objects and events around you. In short...

❍ **The only experience you have of anything is yourself.**

Look out of the window right now look at the view. There is no one alive now or who has lived or who will ever live who will ever experience what you are experiencing now. Even if there is a person standing next to you and they are a friend, close partner, soul mate, twin or clone, your experience is unique to your bias as theirs is unique to their bias.

❍ **All you are able to experience is yourself.**

This is a huge leap in understanding and is the difference between those people that can and cannot solve their problems. Once I realise that I am responsible for my own experience, I have the power to do something about it and I cease to be a victim of circumstance. The words 'response' and 'respond' are from the same route. It is only in *accepting that I am responsible*, that I can become respondable and do something about it. This critical realisation is one that many (if not all) managers and heads of organisations could well embrace as an integral part of their collective and corporate responsibility.

Locating your cupboard

Your cupboard, the place in which you store your unresolved material is located somewhere within your inner house. Somewhere within that self-concept are the cupboards where you hide the material of your unconscious mind. Some cupboards are in the light, upper reaches of the attic and some in the darker recesses of the cellar. The benevolent material is in the attic and the malevolent material in the cellar.

Repressed material, positive or negative, within the unconscious mind affects our every day life. Until we become fully conscious and aware of it and understand it, it remains beyond our control yet we are controlled by it. In a psychological sense, to be controlled often leads to unhappiness. If we are controlled by some inner unresolved emotion or the will of another person, we have lost our self-determination. To be in control often leads to happiness, as we are able to determine our current and future experience. We remain a victim of the unconscious mind until we bring the darkness into the light of the conscious mind and deal with whatever remains unresolved.

The Noble House

The noble house of business, large organisations and institutions also exists within the unconscious minds of those that run them, are employed by them and use them as customers or service users. As with all unconscious connections, the inner experience may differ from the reality of what is actually taking place in the outside world. When a company, seen in the collective unconscious of the population of a country as a pillar of the business community and a solid public institution such as Enron or World.com, takes a nosedive, the whole of society is shaken to some extent or another.

Corporate failure and mismanagement in both public and private sectors can have a devastating effect as evidenced by those jumping from windows after the Wall Street crash. Some companies exist positively in the nation's collective unconscious and are seen in a good light by the general public. For many years, Richard Branson's Virgin Empire has been seen in just such a positive light. Other companies inhabit the darker negative areas of the public collective unconscious. These organisations are tarred with the brush of bad or dodgy dealing. One politician was suspended from the British parliament for two and a half weeks after admitting that he accepted money from Bob Maxwell. In many sections of society, Nestlé will never be forgiven for their policies on the sale of baby milk powder to third world countries, and people I know still avoid Shell petrol stations following their stance on situations in parts of Africa.

The issues that are held in the boxes and bags in the cupboards in our inner house hold feelings, thoughts and attitudes that determine our behaviour. By affecting what we do, these inner repressions effect what will happen to us and where we will end up by controlling what we do or do not pay attention to and dictating what it is that we will accept or reject.

3

Owls In The Attic

You can't have a percept
unless you have a concept

As we go through life we accumulate emotional information and baggage that we store in our unconscious mind. Every time we act in any way, we create a stimulus that affects other people and the universe around us. Each time we create a stimulus, we initiate a response. Our experience of both stimulus and response to our actions creates our understanding of our self and who we are.

The unconscious material held within us dictates our actions and experience. However, this information did not spring out of the ground from nowhere. Somehow, there was a process that led to these concepts becoming a part of our inner unconscious mind. Somehow it got in.

There is a cycle here where experience creates our inner understanding, yet it is our inner understanding that leads us to act and therefore dictates our experience.

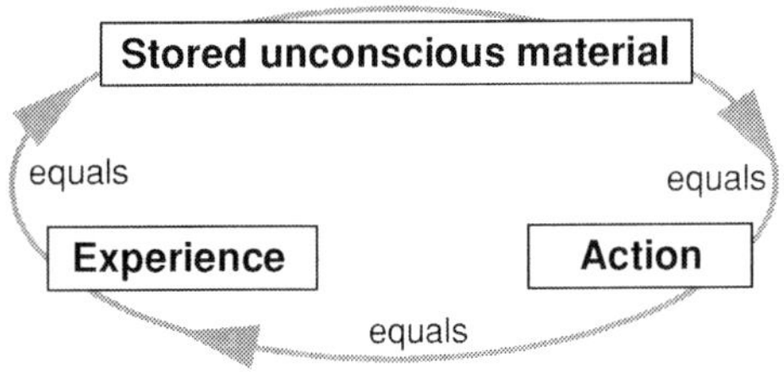

This cycle goes on, unless we wake up to what is happening, below our conscious awareness. We have lots of names that we use to describe what happens to us such as fortune, destiny, luck, fate, karma, the will of god and so on. Whatever the name, the cycle remains the same.

This can begin to sound like a paradox. Well, it is though it is true to say that the experiences we have are dictated directly by the material held in the boxes of our unconscious mind. Hence the description of the inner house is in essence a self-description. Likewise, the way in which we act reinforces and confirms the material held in the unconscious mind. So the unconscious leads us to act and the result of our actions is stored within us. Everything that we do is self descriptive, whom we interact with and who we choose not to interact with, how we dress, how we speak, how we eat, every thing we do is a self description. The relationship between what we hold inside ourselves and what we perceive outside of ourselves is an issue we must develop – but first let us examine our need to store information.

Gathering concepts

From an early age, we begin to gather information. The one thing that we can be sure of is that everyday there will be something new for us to assimilate. There are news broadcasts, the latest episode of our favourite soap, the joke someone told us at lunchtime and that new computer programme at work. There are adverts blasted at us, information about who won the world cup and this year's open golf tournament, new governmental laws and club rules, tests to pass, examination to study for, the changing economy, September the eleventh and scares about anthrax. To each piece of news and every bit of information there will be issues of storage. Some will be practical: 'how do I work this computer programme?' Others will be emotional responses to what we are experiencing: 'how do I tell him I no longer want to see him?'

For most people, we find that, with the amount of emotional material they are experiencing, cupboards are simply too small. It is probable that just a couple of hundred years ago with less information to deal with, a small bag would have been sufficient storage for our inner baggage. The inner bag over time and necessity has become the inner box, and then the inner trunk, cupboard, rooms, and so on. The one thing we know is that the space required to store all this experience continues to grow. The problem is that in the modern world, the amount of information we are required to store during our lifetime is immense.

Stress and information

Those who question 'does stress really exist?' often look at stress as the negative results of the amount of hours we work – 'time load' – or the amount of work we undertake within that time – 'workload'. It may be true that in Britain we work more hours than anyone else in Europe as it is almost certainly true that we pay more and higher taxes than most of our European brothers and sisters, though the amount of hours that we work are not really the point, not the real cause of our stress.

Those poor souls who in the past were the powerhouse of the industrial revolution, worked longer hours in more physically demanding conditions than we ever do now. Those that were sent plummeting in the buttock-clenchingly free-fall of the pithead lift cage to cut coal in the silicosed, ink-black darkness of the mine could justly complain of living in a stressful environment. In the winter, these men, and at times women, went down in the darkness of the unrisen day and returned to the surface into the darkness of an already sunset night and did it at least six days each week. Others worked in mills and factories that blinded, deafened and crippled them. Whatever their workplace, the workers of two hundred years ago went to an earlier and more impoverished grave than we ever would. We now see their lifetimes as ridiculous and the subject of museums and entertainment in kitchen-sink dramas. The fact that stress does exist in modern life is beyond dispute – but our stresses are very different from those of previous generations.

This modern world can be just as stressful and unforgiving as it ever was, though in different ways. To start with, our physical stresses are more to do with sedentary habits. We have become so physically inactive that we have to join clubs and make arrangements, like aerobics classes, to get some exercise. If we do not exercise spontaneously or go to the gym, we can attend 'Mrs Wobble-Bottom's slimming emporium' to be cajoled, bullied and encourage into burning off some unwanted calories or to stop stuffing our faces with unneeded food. Indeed our bodies are under the most tremendous stress of inactivity but even that is not really it. The thing that really sets us apart from all those that have gone before us is information.

I am reminded of when I worked as a gofer for the local council in Brixton, London. Looking back from here, it feels like that time was about one hundred years ago. Anyway, it was when computing was a magic art and all its practitioners were wizards and witches. Seems quite daft now when every spotty kid sports the keyboard reflexes of a martial arts champion. Back in those days, the computer practitioners were the brilliant untouchables who sat at their own table in the staff canteen, spoke a strange and wonderful language and practised their secret arts in the enclosed temple of the computer room, from which all but they were banned. To be acknowledged by one of these Gods was to be touched by a star.

In those days of the nineteen sixties, the average computer system needed an enormous space with a controlled environment. Temperature and humidity had to be maintained at the optimum and the dust eliminated, as this was the computer's greatest enemy. The wizards and witches of this strange art were clothed in their ritual robes of white caps, gowns and gloves that made them look more like modern operating theatre practitioners. The entrance to the temple of the God computer was through two sets of glass doors. The floor space between these two sets of doors was covered by a special type of matting that had the magic property of being able to remove any dirt or dust remaining on the special sterile white shoes. The uninitiated would peer through the glass doors in awe at the wonderful space age scene of whirring tapes and clattering punch card readers – not a screen in sight. The only displays in those days were the endless rolls of computer paper – miles and miles of the stuff. Every infant class and play group within two or three miles of the town hall relied on the supplies of used computer paper so that children could draw and paint on the unprinted under side. Computer suites in those days were big the machines were big, the job was big and so were the egos.

The laptop computer I am using to input this book is several hundred times more powerful than that council computer and is probably several thousand times smaller. Yet inside my laptop are files and folders that hold many thousands times more information than those older computers ever could. The screen and the keyboard of my computer form a portal that is my doorway into a vast suite of rooms built of bits, bytes and megabytes – a bigger space than I could ever hope to fill. It is a land where I am the wizard. I have been initiated into the magic and anytime I wish, I can enter that internal cyber cupboard or suite of rooms. It is as though I have stepped into Doctor Who's Tardis – the space is infinite. This is cyber space, now full of new magic words – such as hacking, hanging, bits, bytes, mega, mouse, hypertext, virus and worm – all newly invented or reinvented.

The unconscious is the computer of the mind

The unconscious mind is not unlike my laptop – there is a lot more to it than meets the eye. It is at the same time very small yet very large. Take a look at the next person you meet. Walk around him or her and take some time to examine the head. How ever bigheaded that person may act, his or her skull is actually really very small. Yet in that head there is a brain and that brain is the connection, the interface to a great tract of inner space, of the unconscious mind. The final frontier is not as Captain Kirk would have us believe with outer space. The final frontier is with these vast unexplored regions of inner space. This is psycho-space. It is here that we find the reality of our boxes and cupboards and discover that we do indeed need a vast amount of psycho-space because we have a lot of information to store. Some people require whole rooms or suites of rooms in which to store their boxes. Our next question is: what is it that is in the boxes – what are we hiding, keeping and storing?

When I go home in the evening I am hit by Harry Potter fever. In every room of the house there are tape machines pouring forth the refined tones of Stephen Fry retelling one or other of the Potter stories. Marie peels the potatoes with a look of concerned intensity as she listens to her favourite book, the Prisoner of Askarban. Simon listens to the 'Chamber of Secrets' in his headphones. His eyes remain distantly unfocussed as he holds the expression of a man who should be in a home for the wretched and confused. The only evidence that serves to confirm he still lives are the odd grunts and smiles issuing from inside the hood of his jacket. His jacket is a disreputable article that seldom seems to leave his back. In my mind I have nicknamed it his kacket rather than jacket – welsh influence there, I think. Amazes me how the boy avoids passing out from the vapours, he wears that many clothes. I mean, who really needs to wear a hood indoors, even at the dinner table. The young are remarkable.

Kate is a beginner in the Potter sagas and at seven years of age, can only cope with the first few tapes of the 'Philosopher's Stone' before it gets a bit scary and then it is, 'can I listen to another story'. I do not know what magic powers Harry Potter has but Mr Fry is imbued with some form of magic of his own that enables him to bring the tales to life through a fine exhibition of verbal animation and dexterity. I am listening to the big book – the one about the Quidich final and amongst the many pictures that Mr Fry manages to paint in my mind, I am rather taken by the one of the owls in the owlery situated at the top of Hogwarts castle. If you have not already been pottered by Mr Fry, it is something that you should rectify immediately. Let me tell you that the owls in the Potter stories are the post service, including parcel post. Any message or article can be sent anywhere using the owls. The magic of the owls is that they are the messengers and can find anybody wherever they are at any time. They both send and return messages. The owls, not surprisingly live in the owlery. This is a huge de-glazed attic at the top of a great tower with many hundreds of birds all of different ages, sizes and colours. Altogether a great diverse, heaving mass of feather and beak attempting both entrance and egress as they go about their errands. There is regurgitated food, owl pellets and droppings all over the place. In fact, the owlery is not dissimilar to my image of the attic contained within the average unconscious mind. .

In the attic of our unconscious mind, are boxes, tea chests, hampers, safes, cupboards, files and envelopes. You name it. All stacked high, all different shapes, sizes and colours, just like the owls. Everything is there. Depending on the owner of the space, the attic will be tidy or a tip. Some attics are organised and well ordered so that required things can be found and retrieved in a trice. Other attics are a higgledy-piggledy shambles where finding something is more likely to be the result of an accident or stunning piece of good fortune. In our attic, whatever state it is in, we store the unconscious evidence we have gathered to enable us to recognise the world around us. As if by owl post, information is brought to the attic and stored in either an organised or disorganised fashion. We store information and facts from our experiences of life. These packets of information tell us about the world and our own attitude towards it and place within it. When we need to retrieve some information, we dip into the attic to extract information from cupboards, boxes and files or wherever we have dumped it. Those whose recall is not so hot, suffer from disorganised attics. There are some personality types who seem to have perfect recall – memories like elephants. Organised attics in their case, I think.

Actually, there are really two areas of storage in the unconscious mind. The attic is more of a reference library in which we keep general information of how our world of experience is structured. Essentially this is a positive collection of useful and useable information rather like an encyclopaedia of knowledge. The altogether darker stuff is held in the cellar. The cellar holds the results of putting the information held in the attic into practice. In short, the attic tells us *who and what we are* while the cellar tells us the *results of our actions* of who and what we are. We will take a look at cellars later, so back to the attic and the question:

How do we know what we know?

How do I know that a dog is a dog?

The first time I saw a dog, either in the flesh or on a page or a screen, I did not know what it was. Dogs and cats all have four legs, two ears and a nose, as do other animals. Somehow, as I discovered the world, I learned to distinguish between cats and dogs so that now I can tell them apart. The strange thing is that I cannot tell you how I do it other than to say this. Somewhere in my attic is a box marked 'Dog'. There is also a box marked 'Cat'. In the dog box, I have stored all the information I need to recognise a dog. Likewise, I have a box containing all the information relating to cats. So that when the conscious mind experiences a cat or dog through the media of the senses, the unconscious mind refers to the correct storage space in the attic to confirm it is a dog and not a cat. This process, though apparently immediate, is actually hugely complex. Dogs come in an infinite variety of sizes, shapes and colours yet I can instantly separate them from cats. My ability to do this exists only because I have stored information in a box in the attic. So that even if a dog has a leg missing or even its head is missing, I am still able to understand that what is being presented to my conscious mind is a dog.

My son Josh, at sixteen months of age, is happily identifying cats as 'meow', ducks as 'quack' and dogs as 'woof'. Already he can identify a variety of representations of duck as 'quack'. We have half a dozen on the pond, which gives him a bit of a start. These real life specimens bear little relationship to the bright yellow plastic ones with bright red and orange beaks that bob in his bath or the Donald represented in a Disney cartoon. But he can recognise the different ducks, drakes and ducklings all as 'quack'. He can also distinguish the goose as 'honk'. So, somewhere in his developing attic, is a box marked 'Duck' – or, in his case, 'Quack' – that enables him to distinguish between ducks and chickens, ducks and geese or ducks and ironing boards.

Cherries are not the only fruit

In our attic we develop and store the information we need to understand the world though there will always be new experiences for which we need to develop a new container.

> I was born in the London inner-city area of Brixton. At the age of four, we moved to a new council house in Roehampton. The estate was thrown down between the open spaces of Putney Heath, Wimbledon Common and Richmond Park. There were no boxes for the countryside in my attic. As an infant, my only experience was the inner city. To accommodate the open space of the country, new boxes had to be filled. My first new experience out of the inner city was when I went with my mother and father to visit the house prior to the move. In the garden, I found a conker or horse chestnut – no box for that. The nearest box available in my attic was one with 'Cherry' written on it. I had seen cherries in the big fruit market in Brixton though I had no memory of tasting one. So I decided that this conker must be a cherry and tried to eat the conker much to the amusement of all those around me. Little children learn quickly so that once the 'Conker' box had been established in its rightful place in the attic, it becomes filled with pickling techniques, drilling holes, baking in the oven, cheese cutters, string, sore knuckles and all the paraphernalia associated with conkers. From that day onwards, I have not confused a cherry with a conker.

For some, rice pudding and sex are bed fellows

All that we recognise out there is only recognisable because we recognise it in here. The process is more complex so that at an early age, we start to develop boxes for complex emotions. Concepts such as love may require several boxes, physical love, friendship love, sibling love, children love etc, all similar though different enough to require their own box. If the boxes are in some way jumbled so that sexual love and children love become merged, we see the development of the paedophile. In this case, when the senses perceive a child out there, an internal connection is made to the sexuality box in here. Paedophiles' boxes may have become mixed in their childhood so that the abused become the abusers. If, therapy is to be successful in these cases, the boxes need to be unpacked and separated so that the connections are broken.

The same process may happen and connect the sexual box with the violence box or, come to that, the sexual box with the rice pudding box. Whatever the mix is, the associating is established so that you 'can't have one without the other'. If a connection has been made between sexual activity and rice pudding, the person my find it impossible to respond sexually unless the rice pudding is present. Equally, packets of rice pudding on the supermarket shelf might lead to hot flushes and quickened heartbeats. As attics become muddled, then odd or dysfunctional connections can be made that may take us out of the norm and lead us to be seen as eccentric, weird or perverted.

Cognitive and emotional boxes

When it comes to boxes in the attic, the movement, reallocation or assimilation of structural or cognitive material is relatively easy. We can be taught the theory of anything and file it away for later reference. On the other hand, in general we do not find it so easy to learn emotional things. We seldom learn emotionally from the experience of others. It is difficult to create and fill emotional boxes from what others tell us or teach us. Sadly and often painfully, we only truly know an emotional thing by doing it our self. In a cognitive or academic sense, we can store information in the attic from what we read or learn. I know that China exists though I have never been there. In my attic is a box labelled China that incorporates some intimate information, ideas and statistics. This box remains limited because, whatever I know cognitively, I do not know what it feels like to be in China. It may be that a skilful story, book or film may give an emotional impression. It may even move me very deeply and I may include these feelings in my China box but it is all second hand experience. The writer of the story is processing their experience into their boxes and then reinterpreting it into the story. I am also perceiving the story and reprocessing it to fit the boxes in my attic. Like a complex Chinese whisper, the essential image of the story in my attic may bear no resemblance to that held in the attic of the writer. The image in the writer's attic may bear no resemblance to what actually occurred in China.

As so often happens, the information in my box is refracted and distorted through the experience, bias and prejudice of others and as such may be only fantasy, having only the faintest flirtation with the truth. Yet I may believe that I hold valid knowledge about China and begin to make definitive statements as though they are real facts. 'It is a known fact that…' I may be talking absolute nonsense, yet believe that these opinions are valid. All the time I may be unaware of my ignorance because the knowledge and information is stored below my awareness in the boxes of the unconscious mind. I often wonder when I hear people making comments across racial, social and religious barriers as though it is possible to really understand what life is like for other people. Is it possible for a black person born in Droitwich to understand what it is like to be a black person in a village in the out-back of Africa? Just as it must be pretty difficult for a white man born in New York to understand what life is like for a white man born in South Africa. I am amazed when men make assumptions about what it is like to be female or equally when a woman comments inappropriately about what it is like to be a man. We are all limited by the contents of our boxes and, unless we know this, not only do we remain ignorant but remain ignorant of our ignorance and cease to learn.

❍ Just because I experience something or believe something, it does not follow that it is so.

It is only by being prepared to open and update our internal boxes that we can hope to grow as people.

A bit of psycho-speak

These inner understandings or concepts that we build of the universe we inhabit are known in psycho-speak as *internal working models.*

❍ You can't have a percept unless you have a concept.

I can only perceive that what I am experiencing out there, through my senses, is a dog because I have the concept of what a dog is in here in my 'dog' box. No dog box, no concept. No concept, no percept. I do not know what it is. To understand what it is, I need to fill a box. I need an internal working model of a dog as my concept.

The dog in my head

Internal working models of external objects have been an accepted part of developmental psychology for many years. Particularly used in the analytical school, they begin to explain how our perception works. I hold within me a model of things and feelings, hopes and attitudes, expectations and desires. So, along with the internal working model of the dog I have an entire menagerie of beasties and birdies, people and places, objects, feelings and things.

Internal working models are concepts in boxes

Our recognition of objects, animals and other people can be fairly easily understood as the contents we hold in a labelled box. If what is out there matches up with what I hold in my box, I know what it is. There are various complex and partly emotional boxes that are less easily understood. Such as the boxes we should consider that we hold in our attic containing roles that we are committed to enact. These may be such things as social or intellectual roles or may be as fundamental as those labelled 'Man' or 'Woman'. The details of the gender role that we have stored in our box are built from observation, media, books, stories, expectation, direct interactive experience and genetics. The manner in which we manifest our sense of gender is totally an expression of our box contents.

As a man, I have inner assumptions of how I should or should not act. There are things that I should or should not do. The contents of my 'Man' box are very specific. There are details of how I should treat women and other men, details of fidelity and sexuality, attitudes to violence and love, the expression of feelings, what is manly and what is not. There are body details about long and short hair, facial hair, nasal hair, ear hair etc. The minutia of intimate behaviour and sexual intimacy, attitudes to genitals, whether or not it is better to have a foreskin or be circumcised and which is the best way to wipe one's backside. It is all in there in the box.

Because the boxes are filled, or begin to be filled early in our existence, we have little memory of not having a concept of something or the need to make some sense of the unknown. As adults, the speed at which we retrieve information and confirm our experience can lead us to believe that the box does not exist because we have become complacent and fail to understand how we know what we know. You see, in my attic, I have boxes marked with your name, 'the reader'. In those boxes are concepts that I hold about you. Some of the detail will be true, the remainder will be my bias and fantasy. The information is detailed and may include my assumed information about your most intimate behaviour.

Of course, none of it may be true. That is the magic of the unconscious and the question of how do we know that anything we experience is real or true? The answers to such questions can only be addressed when we wake up to what is happening within us so that we start to become active participants in life rather than simply being observers.

The things that are true about individuals are also true about businesses, companies and all organisations.

The unconscious organisational self-concept (OSC)

The people that live and work inside an organisation all play a part in the creation and maintenance of the whole being. The people participating in any organisation or group are like the cells that make up any organ in the human body. Each cell has an effect on the organ and equally the organ as a whole has an effect on each individual cell. The function of an organ is the reason it exists, the 'why are we here'? The cells of the pancreas remain true the organ. They do not try to be a heart or a kidney. If a cell in an organ decides to go against the collective functions of the organ and develops a separate way of doing its own thing, we call it a tumour or a cancer. Such cells may be benign and simply impede the process of the organ. They may be or become malignant and threaten the very existence of the organ.

As with organs, every organisation has a function or purpose. This is the organisational self-concept and is maintained below the conscious awareness of the people in the organisation. The people, like cells, create the whole organisation that works, provided that each individual submits to the OSC. If individuals go against the OSC, they become a cancer that works against the wellbeing of the whole. In the end, the rogue employees need to be cut out or they will seriously damage the organisation. Barings Bank became fatally damaged by the rogue trader Nick Leeson, who developed his own concept of what should be happening and in so doing separated himself form the wellbeing of the whole. The bank was only saved through being the subject of a take-over.

The organisational self-concept may be at odds with the mission statement

The OSC is working at an unconscious level. On the other hand, mission statements and organisational objectives are conscious. The two may not be the same thing and may work against each other. The OSC should not become confused with the mission statement or managerial ideals. The mission statement is about what we would like to be or how we would like others to see us. The organisational self-concept (OSC) is about what we actually are. When the OSC and the organisational objective are the same, the organisation has achieved a state of organisational enlightenment. This is very rare.

Understanding the OSC is difficult for those within it. They are too close to it to have any objective understanding. It is the independent consultant who is able to develop a clear view of the OSC. Often the new employee also can see what is going on in the organisation, although in time all new staff will be absorbed into the OSC and see it as the status quo and as it should be. If we do attempt to understand the OSC, we need to employ other words to describe it such as 'organisational ethos', 'our style of doing things', 'our management style', 'our informal approach to employee relations' and so on.

The average OSC will take years to develop. Once it has been established, it is difficult to change. Firstly, the people with the power in the organisation do not realise that it exists and need to understand it and accept its consequences. If this is a negative OSC based in bullying or negative management styles, there may be a lot of resistance to accepting that it exists at all. Whether it is recognised or not, the OSC does exists and it does have an effect on all those within the organisation and all those that use the organisation. The development of the OSC, unless it has been carefully and deliberately managed, will grow organically over time. Often, the middle managers will learn the OSC from higher managers. This will rarely happen through organised training but is more likely the product of being treated in a certain way by those above which is then passed on down the organisation. There will also be the effect of observation, seeing how higher managers operate. As someone says in one of the Harry Potter books,

'If you want to understand the measure of a man, observe how he treats his inferiors, not his equals.'

In most organisations, there is almost always an inferior to be kicked if that is the style of the OSC. It does not have to be that way. We can develop positive and caring OSCs. We simply need the will and determination to change, see it through and develop positive attitudes and behaviours.

4

Generations and Self-concepts

When you share a concept, you belong.

The experience of childhood differs with each generation. Generally, across any one country, the experience for those growing up at a certain time will be similar. Each generation creates its own reference points that define their era. There are shared references to popular music, celebrity personalities and stars, television and radio programmes, series, soaps, books, fashions and so on. Each reference point becomes a shared concept in the collective unconscious of each generation. Some of these famous people and events will be made into icons that signify that particular time in history.

Currently the image of aeroplanes flying into the twin towers of the World Trade Centre in New York will probably become visual icons of this age. Many children growing up now will remember the significance of Harry Potter long after the books go out of print. The image of Che Guevara is evocative of the freedom fighter or terrorist, depending on your point. For many, the image of John Lennon and Yoko Ono evoke memories of the peace movement. Any icon is more than the simple image or sound. When we see or hear an icon, the image or sound is really the key that opens the conceptual box in our unconscious that contains all the emotional connections that we have made to that time or era. Many of these connections will be to specific remembered events, relationships or personalities. In virtually all cases, the individual significance of an icon is greater than the icon itself. Che Guevara might have been a total bastard or an angel – I simply do not know. Though I do know the psychological impact of the image in the famous poster of Che in his beret printed in black against a red background. It was standard kit for the sixties rebel, viewed mainly through the smoky haze of slowly combusting grass, resin and joss sticks. He was a personality of the time even if that personality was created and maintained by the media. As personalities, Sinatra, Buddy Holly, Elvis, the Beatles, Oasis, Robbie Williams and so on, symbolise the youth of that generation. The songs that they and others sing create an immediate link to boxes of concepts and boxes of memories stored in our unconscious mind. Famous people become icons of the times.

Iconoclasts have power

An iconoclast is the person who breaks down the deeply held and cherished images of past generations. An icon is both a totem of the era it embodies and a destroyer of the preceding icons, although there are some images and icons that spread beyond their generation. A silhouette of Queen Victoria can evoke the attitudes of the Victorian era – 'we are not amused'. A main icon of the First World War has to be the posters of Lord Kitchener pointing out of the billboard barking at you that you are needed to die in battle for Queen and country – 'your country needs you'. All the issues of the Second World War can be evoked by the picture of Winston Churchill with his curiously bent back holding his outrageously large cigar, offering his two fingers that were raised in a salute of victory.

As with iconoclastic people, iconoclastic products and their advertised images and slogans tend to be era-specific and may be meaningless to people from generations before or after. New products displace previously important ones. The image of compact discs overtook the vinyl record just as DVDs are taking over videotape and VHS overtook Betamax. There is a battle between re-recordable CDs and the mini disc. The battle is not between the products. The only real task the manufacturer needs to face is to win the battle to fix a new concept in the collective unconscious. What we see as the thing to buy, whether or not it is better, is the one we will buy and that product will therefore succeed. This is never truer than in the case of fashion.

Fashions date the wearer

Clothing looks dated because each season we are subject to new images in the fashion shows that give us new concepts that finally feed down into the high street stores. So, each year, the colour of choice changes and skirt lengths rise and fall. Shirt collars become longer or shorter and the number of buttons on a suit jacket are more or fewer. I always thought I was above all that. I can remember, when bell-bottom trousers hit the streets, saying clearly that I would not be seen dead in them. A year later, I was alive and well and wearing bell-bottoms. Actually, they were hipster bell-bottoms that, with the addition of a wide-brimmed hat, made me look like a mushroom.

Somewhere along the line, a bright spark or pervert in the fashion world decided that we would all enjoy displaying the names of people, products and organisations on our clothing. I seem to recall an outburst of sweatshirts sporting the logos and mottos of various American Universities. Why on earth someone from Chipping Sodbury would want to wear a garment advertising the wares of an educational establishment in Ohio I have no way of knowing. Now we see sweatshirts dedicated to 'Fred Bloggs', 'Ralph Lauren' or that all too suggestive 'FCUK', and every other self-opinionated organisation everywhere.

I can remember taking James at age fourteen to buy a pair of trainers. He was a size twelve then, so getting any pair was pretty hard. Once the limiting factor of trainers of that size with the appropriate name on the side was taken into account, finding a pair became mission impossible. His self-concept demanded that he should have a pair with a fashionable name on the side and then his trainers would fit within the concept that he shared with his friends, so that he would feel as though he belonged. A nation-wide search needed to be undertaken to find trainers in his size. They look more like canoes than

> shoes, and then, at the point of my total despair, in the back of a sports shop in Chester, a smiling assistant produced a pair with 'Nike' plastered all over them. Apparently, the wrong colour, but beggars can't be choosers or, in this case, people with big feet put up with what they can get. They were in the bag and away before you could say: 'I don't like that pair, can we go somewhere else'. Mind you, at the price they were asking, we needed a mortgage! Pity the poor single parent.

You have to hand it to them – what a clever concept. Not only do we all walk around being free advertising boards, but also we pay premium prices for the privilege. The ultimately clever part of the trick however, is that we feel that we are obliged to buy the things in the first place. As with clothes, go the fashions in living accessories in colour, style and decoration both in and out of the house. The kitchen makeovers and bathroom makeovers are quickly followed by the garden makeover. The phenomenon of what used to be known as 'keeping up with the Jones's' has moved from a social focus to an economically driven force that is powered not just by business but also by media. Society has moved in the fifty-one years of my lifetime from concepts such as: 'you're lucky to have a pair of shoes at all', to 'I refuse to have any shoes unless they are those ones there and no others will do'. The demands of the young have become the bane of every parent – especially the single parent – and the boon to the banks and credit card companies that fund it all. We now inhabit a social landscape in which even cars, mobile phones and laptop computers are made to look and be fashion accessories. We accept and absorb the concept and need to be seen to be branded. It might be Fcuk, BMW, RR, Aga or whatever on everything from sweatshirts to key fobs – each becomes a social icon of the times.

Generational images cut across social and economic boundaries

In any age, there will always be a variety of experience in different geographical areas of any country. Social groups are separated by levels of poverty and prosperity that dictate people's ease of access to any of these generational icons. Equally there will be a variation in what we Brits tend to describe, as 'class', which also creates the sense of difference in access financially and socially to all that any age has to offer. Whatever the geography or class, each era has its own flavour that distinguishes it from what has been and what is yet to come. As an icon becomes set, the cheaper imitations rush in to cash in on the impoverished lower end of the market. So that if we were born into the 'Filofax' era and needed to be seen to be carrying one, we could chose the genuine and expensive article in genuine hand brushed buck skin or settle for one of a thousand of similar though cheaper imitations is cold hard PVC.

Whether we shop at Harrods or Ethel Austin's, we will find different makes of the same style and product in each shop. We all need to feel that we belong by complying with the fashion trends of our time and group. If you do not believe me, go and look at some photographs of yourself ten or twenty years ago – I bet you'll laugh. The collective experience of each generation creates a collective generational or societal ethos not unlike the company ethos that we examined in the previous chapter. The ethos becomes embedded in the collective unconscious of that generation, creating a generational self-concept or GSC. The manner in which any generation perceives itself will be to a great extent dependent on the concepts held in the collective unconscious of the population at that time. Many of those concepts will be given or nurtured into the conceptual boxes while others will be instinctual or genetic and be in the box anyway.

The GSC determines the way in which one generation treats the next. In this way, the sins of the fathers are truly visited on the sons. The GSC describes how we as a society treat each other and what is and is not acceptable. Issues such as the age of consent and general attitudes to both sexual activity and sexual orientation are very much products of the prevailing GSC. The GSC dictates acceptable social behaviour, as do the laws ruling the dealings of the financial community or the Commission for Racial Equality.

Violence can be a form of communication

When I was a child, in the 1950s in Brixton, our parents, the previous generation, had lived through the experience and the difficulties of the global economic depression of the 1930s. Many of them suffered the indignities and desperation of poverty, unemployment, homelessness and soup kitchens and in the extreme, real starvation in the depression. Following on the heels of the depression came the six years of the trauma and depravations of the Second World War from 1939 to 1945. In 1951, the year of my birth, rationing, a product of wartime survival, was still alive and well and attitudes of using everything you had and not wasting anything were prevalent. This was a continual horror to me as the 'hand me down' culture of the time meant that I was at the end of a line that received clothing from my sisters. Some of the jumpers and trousers I was made to wear were a total embarrassment, especially the colours.

My mother clothed us all by going to jumble sales and buying articles such as jumpers and cardigans. These would then be unpicked. I was made to stand with my arms outstretched while the wool was wound first into hanks and then into balls. For my youngest sister Karen, my mother constructed a woollen masterpiece that had the face of a large rag doll on the front. This had long blond hair made from loose wool and buttons for eyes. When this was handed down, I looked nothing short of a prat, and so all my chums reminded me. The jumpers, the crew-cut and the national health glasses held on with elastic so that I did not break them, were all icons of poverty but also of that time – I was not alone. 'Prats are us' as they say.

With the continued rationing, there were limits on what we could buy to eat or buy to wear. As far as I recall, rationing did not finish until 1953 or 1954. Beyond the limitations imposed by rationing then and the general GSC of poverty, there was a subtler, unspoken GSC of the time. This was that violence was an acceptable form of communication. I suppose in a world where a whole generation of men have come back from years of prolonged killing and fighting, it would only be natural to assume that the new concepts of their learned behaviour would lead them to carry these attitudes on into the society to which they returned. Their behaviour may have been moderated somewhat to fit into a civilian world, though the attitudes remained rooted in the violence of armed conflict. To strike out at those that annoyed or created upset had become, for many, instinctual.

Domestic violence perpetrated by the man as the undisputed head of the house who ruled the roost, as the leader of the family, was a common part of my early life. Not just in my own home but also as part of the society I grew up in. Outside of the home, violence was an accepted part of everyday life. At infants' school, we were slapped on the backside. At primary school, a tall, cruel man called Mr Grey would call us out in front of the school for talking or some other minor misdemeanour. He would pull up the trouser leg and administer a hard slap to the outside of the thigh giving what was termed in those days as a 'dead leg'. This would often happen on the stage at the morning assembly. The public display on the stage added an extra twist to the punishment, using the victim's public humiliation as a lesson to the whole school to deter other would-be transgressors. At secondary school, in the class room, the favoured weapon of the teachers was the ruler across the palm. If a teacher really desired to produce, pain the knuckles would be the chosen point of impact.

At secondary school, my English master introduced himself to the class on the first day by shouting at us, 'If you're good blokes, I'm a good bloke, too. If not, I'm a BASTAAARD!' It was not unknown for him to throw a projectile at a non-attentive pupil. Whistling through the air would fly a piece of chalk or if he was in a more energetic mood the board rubber. The board rubber was a heavy article about nine inches long made of wood with a felt pad stuck on one side. If you were lucky, the felt pad hit you first. This was a vicious weapon when thrown accurately – and he could – across the classroom. A good shot would 'smack you upside the ear' as they used to say.

Such open displays of violent hostility were the norm in most classrooms. One particular maths teacher set his class out in single desks. He would prowl the rows while terrified pupils wrestled with a mathematical conundrum. At the slightest opportunity, the teacher would lift a child, male or female, from the chair by pulling the hairs at the top of the side burn near the ear. Using this particular form of torture, he would painfully march children around the room whilst attempting to humiliate them in front of their peers. For serious transgressions, a more thorough beating was called for. Children would be sent to their housemaster or mistress. The boys were disciplined with a cane and girls with a slipper. As the ultimate deterrent, the chap who really knew how to whip the cane was Mr George, the deputy head, who ruled the school by fear. When Mr George retired, the role was taken over by an Australian gym teacher called Mr Blue. One of his roles, doubtless not in his job description, was to discipline the bigger, rougher boys who no one else could handle. All the schools I attended had that aura of fear about them that kept everyone 'in line'. Such concepts of violence being acceptable were passed on down to us children. Bullying, fighting and violent or dangerous games were normal.

Everyone acted as though they were your parent

Even outside of school, we were never really free from the chastisement of adults. When mucking about in public or playing the fool in the street, it would not be uncommon for any adult to give you a 'mouthful', a 'smack' or a 'boot up the backside'. It is also true that the local policeman, who appeared on his pushbike and then later on one of those funny, grey, water-cooled scooter-motorbike things, would just as easily give you a kick. This was never considered an assault or an offence against our human rights; the concepts that we had any rights at all had not yet been invented.

Much of a child's interaction with adults at that time was moderated by 'respect'. We were taught to respect our 'elders' or act as though we did, even if we did not. We were encouraged to see them as our 'betters'. We knew that if the policeman had taken us home, or if a letter had been sent home from our school complaining of our bad behaviour, that our father's punishment would probably be a lot worse than any that we had been given so far. We therefore kept our mouths firmly shut. This was a time when the behaviour of children was modified by violence and fear. Such concepts allowed the development of what we now know as abuse. Children simply did not have a voice as they do now.

That does not mean that we felt badly done to or that we lay awake in fear of our lives. It was simply that 'that' was the way things were. It was normal to be physically punished whether you deserved it or not. There was both the fear of being punished and the fear of being humiliated. This was after all a time when hanging, beating and flogging were legal and considered as acceptable forms of corporal punishment, when homosexuality was illegal and the age of adulthood was twenty one – key to the door and all that. The sixties had not yet begun.

Pass the parcel

Of course our parents were only passing on the concepts they had inherited from their parents and their own life experience. Their parents, and their parents before them, had been playing pass the parcel with violent concepts for generations. Our grandfathers were those men that had survived the ravages of the First World War. They had the concept of violence beaten into their conceptual boxes by Victorian parents who had survived previous wars in building and maintaining the British Empire. As the parcel was passed on, the parents continued to beat the violent concepts given to them into their own children. My grandparent's generation were often chastised as a matter of course – 'spare the rod and spoil the child', 'this will hurt me more than it hurts you'. The privileges of children were few. Children were 'seen and not heard' with virtually no rights in society or in law. The verbal expressions of such concepts have cascaded down the generations.

'Do you want me to wipe that stupid smile off your face?'

'Don't do what I do, do what I tell you?'

'Shut up or I'll give you something to cry about.'

'I'll swing for you.'

'I'll give you a thrashing you'll never forget.'

'I'll knock you into the middle of next week.'

My favourite was my Grandmother who always threatened to 'bash me bandy' – something I still do not understand. The strangest thing is that, once a generation has accepted a concept, they will embrace and support it. Those that meted out the physical punishment to us had experienced the same thing. They justified their behaviour by making statements such as;

'It never did me any harm.'

There were boxes and boxes held in the inner attics of our great grandparents our grandparents and our parents that were full of the unconscious baggage of violence. In many cases, our parents passed these concepts on to us. Maintaining the same tradition, some of us have passed them on to our children. In their turn, a percentage of our children will pass them on to their next generation. The violent concepts that we hold are not only the results of violence but also the perpetuators of violence. So, if I am beaten sufficiently, I will take on board the concept that to act violently is normal and acceptable behaviour. This concept will create a relative percept that serves to reinforce the concept so that it becomes acceptable for me to act violently also.

The same principles are true for such things as child abuse so that negative concepts are passed from one generation to the next. Just like the children's party game 'pass the parcel', these accepted attitudes of negative behaviour are passed on until someone stops and opens the box. When an individual decides to open a box and reorganise the contents, we use words like psychotherapy, analysis and counselling. When a group of people decide to reorganise a box, we use words like a sect, a fad, an 'ism or an 'ology, heresy, terrorism or revolution. When an entire generation decides to reorganise a box, we use words like a 'movement', 'social change' or the 'evolution of ideas'.

The lovely revolution

Do you remember the hippies? Whatever your feelings are about flower power and the hippy movement of love peace and happiness, we have to accept that the movement was about the actions of young westerners attempting to reject the outmoded concepts held by their parents. Every generation wants to do it, not all can. Some thought this to be evolution whilst others felt it was a revolution. In the main, flower power was a truly unconscious event conducted mainly below the awareness of those involved. Flower power described a generation attempting to reorganise its generational self-concept in such a way as to make it significantly different from those GSCs that had gone before.

We may not now live in the land of milk and honey, peace and happiness, promised by the hippy movement. Wars are probably just as prevalent as they ever were even if they are, in the main, fought at arm's length, using smart weapons rather than by hand-to-hand fighting. The outcome today of the love and peace movement of the sixties is that we do live in a significantly different atmosphere from those of previous generations. We now live in a world where people, including children, have rights enshrined in law that they have not had before. There continues to be a liberalisation of social rules and taboos backed up by the European court of human rights and the social chapter. We have family and children's courts. Issues such as child abuse have tumbled from their hiding place in the collective unconscious. Our collective concepts have changed so that these things are now open topics for discussion. Television programmes now overtly show sexual activity and people openly discuss bodily functions and diseases such as bowel cancer. Adverts encourage us to buy the best medicines and creams to heal thrush. Sanitary towels and panty liners with added wings fly across the television screen. Times have changed. Times will continue to change because concepts change and as concepts change, the percepts follow.

Changing male gender concepts

From the sixties onwards, there has been a relaxation of attitudes to behaviour, dress, social, sexual, business and moral etiquette. This is perceived in one sense as a good thing. The scruffy, under-dressed, greasy-Brylcreem-haired male of the 1940s has been replaced with the sweet-smelling, smooth-shaven, hair-gelled man of the millennium. The belt and braces gave way to a softer and altogether more tender look. At some point, there was a dramatic change and suddenly men looked and dressed in a less macho, more feminine style. Looking smart and casually smart equalled attractiveness. Men started using cosmetics and even began to wear jewellery. Watches, rings and bracelets glittered. The sixties male wore strings of beads and bells.

Currently men may even wear more jewellery than their women folk, especially of the pierced variety. Whether it is the brightly coloured cocks-comb of the punk rocker or the flamboyant dress of Lawrence whatever-his-name-is, as he goes about changing rooms, it is now acceptable to be openly expressive in a way that it never was before. It is okay to be yourself, no longer confined by the rigid structure of the previous GSC. We have moved beyond the previous confines. It is only when we develop the ability to open our conceptual boxes that we are able to find a route to change and a sense of free self-expression. For this to come about, society has had to learn to question existing concepts. The greatest contributors to these changes in British national self-concept were probably the two World Wars.

It can take big events to change small concepts

From both World Wars, men returned from facing death and depravation in situations where they had mixed with other men from differing social groups. When people began to realise that they were not any better or worse than those people in other social classes, then the barriers began to be dismantled. It would be foolish to claim that there are no social barriers left in Britain. In some areas they are alive and well, though in general, society is less diverse and is becoming homogenised. We are developing a standardisation by virtue of what we are shown by the media, advertising and, these days, the internet. The ability to question the current GSC only develops when the time is right and then society can take a change in direction.

It is only when I am in a setting where I am allowed to be myself that I have the opportunity to expand and enjoy my own self-concept. If I can play with my concepts, I am able to experiment with ideas. In discovering my true self-concept, I can enjoy financial, emotional and sexual freedoms and so on. Experimenting and playing with my self-concept is something that is in many ways has been the province of adolescence. The acceptance of change in general and the drive to personal change and development is something that is now shared by people of all ages, as the high rate of divorce would testify. In my clients, I now detect that the questioning and experimentation has moved up the age scale. In some parts of the country, the age group most likely to report to the genito-urinary clinic is the over sixty-fives. The permissive society has arrived at last for some, at least.

For the more conservative lay and professional psychological and social commentators, these changes in GSC are seen as a bad thing. Moves towards liberalisation threaten the current order and the general status quo. Most people do not like change or the threat of change. Currently, the country is attempting to change its fiscal concept to adopt the Euro. To do this, the country will need to rid itself of the concept that the Pound is a sacrosanct icon. From the changing attitudes in the press, this does seem to be happening. I now suspect that in a year or so we will all be spending Euros and the Pound will become something that we tell the children about.

I note that in the news over the last couple of weeks that the USA and the British government are both attempting to change or develop our concepts of Iraq. It would appear that the object of the exercise is to change our concept in such a way as to make the bombing of the Iraqi people or an all out war against them an acceptable option.

The changing female gender concept

As the male concepts have made the long journey from violence to semi-communication and mild states of sensitivity, the female gender concepts have made the journey from dependence to semi-independence. Women that stay in relationships these days are more likely to do so because they want to rather than because they need to. I know abuse exists and some women remain emotionally trapped or addicted to a negative situation but choices now exist that were never a part of the previous female gender concept. Women have power. There is support beyond the man of the house and in many cases women no longer need men at all other than to provide sperm to reproduce. The increasing divorce rate, I note with my clients at least, is driven by women and their unwillingness to accept what their mothers put up with. The concept of who they are, how they should be treated by men and their general rights have developed and grown. In the vast majority of cases, it is the woman who decides when the relationship is at an end. Women no longer need men for support. The law would seem to have followed this move. At the point of split, the new laws favour the women and her (not their) children so that in most cases, the marital home is really the property of the women and children, not the man. His percentage of financial ownership in law may be very small indeed.

As gender concepts change, we find men needing to work harder to get and keep a woman. Subsequently, men are cleaner, better groomed, use more cosmetics and generally work harder at attracting the opposite sex than previous generations did. Every changing concept has a price in terms of the changed percept. Men can now be the objects of sexual voyeurism by women and seen as pinups or simply viewed as sexual objects. Previously, men that got around sexually were seen as 'a bit of a lad' while women who got around were seen as 'old bikes'. Currently, I would say that most of my female clients seem much more aware of their own sexuality. They are not afraid to make the first move, to ask a man out, buy them flowers or be sexually open; something many men find disquieting, I often notice. It is not uncommon for women to openly admit to wanting a good 'shag', a word used much more by women than men. Women are now more likely to take sexual control and use a man just as men have in the past used women – women on top and all that.

The economic revolution

Much of the change in the gender concepts as described above has only been possible through a general increase in the wealth of Western society. The previous concepts of poverty are in the main no longer with us. Even members of our society that we might consider as poor, such as single parents, are profoundly better off than their forebears. As citizens of a wealthy country, we can benefit from the products and services that apparently make our lives easier. Even those that might be considered as poor have televisions, videos and mobile phones as a staple necessity. We can now travel in comfort on our foreign holidays and experience the relative poverty of less well-off peoples and further enjoy our sense of wealth.

The perceptions of ourselves as wealthy are relatively new. Behind the percepts are new concepts that have not been held by previous generations. These changing concepts of us include the possibility and potential for change. We expect to better ourselves and to accumulate possessions and wealth in the form of pensions and insurance (provided that interest rates are maintained) and that great British institution, the house or castle. We have greater expectation than ever before. We are no longer interested in the concepts of mere survival that belonged to previous generations. We want concepts of improved quality of our survival – we expect things to get progressively better. We want to follow these concepts with perceptions of our own wealth. For past generations concepts of life were much more cautious

'...you do not have anything until you can afford to pay for it.'

Without social support, dole or whatever they call it these days, being out of work or in debt would have led to disaster and possible homelessness. It is not that long ago that people who were in debt could end up in the 'workhouse'. A major social development after the Second World War was the provision of financial and health support. It is only when we know that we will be supported if things go wrong that we can allow ourselves to take on debt. In modern

Britain, we use our flexible friends to allow us to enjoy the future in the present, courtesy of the credit card companies. The concept has changed from 'have it when you can afford it' to 'buy now, pay later'.

Gender in the workplace

There is much talk in business of glass ceilings and the limitations put on women in the workplace, especially in management structures. It is easy to get stuck in the gender concepts, woman as nurses, men as soldiers, men as managing directors, women as personnel officers. Most of these role archetypes are being challenged and many knocked over. I noticed today that the breaking gender role story is that women in the British armed forces are trained in the same way as male soldiers under the equal opportunities banner and sustain greater rates of physical injury. The commentator presented this as though it was a great surprise.

We can probably all accept that, despite our psychological concepts and expectations, men's and women's bodies are different and subsequently there will be activities that are better performed by one sex rather than the other. That does not mean that these activities cannot be done by either gender, simply one may be better at it than the other – some roles are gender-specific. The concept that a man with one leg is unable to run a mile is patently wrong. However it cannot be denied that a man with two legs is likely to perform the task quicker and with greater ease. In the changing societal concept towards political correctness, it is easy to overlook this. The bottom line is that some people are better at some things than others.

As you read this and review your own concepts, keep this point in mind. Just because you *can* do something, it does not follow that you *should* do it or that you are any good at it. I can plaster a wall but it takes me longer to do a worse job than my mate the builder. Reviewing our concepts requires a certain degree of honesty. A man who has no hair is not follically challenged, he is bald. Just as someone who is over-weight is not lipidly challenged, he is fat and a man of no great height is not vertically challenged, he is short. If you are old you are old, if you are crippled you are crippled. To grow emotionally requires honesty. Never be afraid to call something what it is. There is no need to call something in the way that fashion dictates so that we remain politically correct. To be honest, we need to understand the mechanisms that have filled our boxes – so what is it?

5

Who Put That in My Attic?

Can I make a meal of you?

All our major concepts, those that tell us who we are and how we relate to those around us in the world at large, are set very early on in life. The human system is built to learn. Our senses and the nervous system that processes the information from our senses are all designed to tell us about what is going on in the world around us. This is active at least from the moment of birth so that by the age of three or four, we are fairly set about our gender and identity. Beyond these core concepts of 'self', we continue to grow psychologically, emotionally and mentally. Our ability to develop and change our concepts and percepts is probably the greatest factor in our evolutionary success because it leaves with a legacy of adaptability.

Unlike other animals on the planet, we have a long and extended childhood that really lasts until we are around twenty-five years of age. I can hear a chorus of women looking at their men folk and maintaining that they have never grown up at all. This long childhood allows us to learn like no other animal. The vast strides mankind has made in the last few hundred years have required great changes in concepts to understand the new percepts around us. We have rushed from a labour intensive agricultural technology to an industrial and now digital technology. I think it was Desmond Morris in his book *The Human Zoo* who first made the observation that the man in the cockpit of a jumbo jet or Concorde is actually no different from the man who, a few hundred, or maybe even a few thousand years ago, was driving a horse and cart. Yet the modern perceptual world is vastly different.

In this digital age, I feel that sometimes my basic mechanical thinking hampers me. I was brought up in a mechanical age of levers and pulleys. The high-tech Christmas present in my childhood was a Meccano set. Meccano was the forerunner of Lego that involved metal plates and nuts and bolts to build elaborate working mechanical models. There are times when my mechanical mind cannot conceive the working of digital technology. I mean, I know that when I operate the keys of my computer that characters appear on the screen. It is just that I have no understanding of how they get there. To understand digital technology, I need to build another box in my attic labelled digital concepts and then attend a course that will give some information to put in it.

Building the boxes

It is popular for us human beings to distance ourselves from animals, but we all work the same way. All beings, including animals, create inner concepts to allow them to make sense of their perceptual experience. When an animal meets another animal it has three major questions that it must answer:

Can I eat it?

Does it want to eat me?

Can I mate with it?

These are fairly basic, though crucially important, concepts. Fundamentally, getting these concepts and the percepts right can mean the difference between the survival of a species or becoming a predator's lunch. The processes that allow us to develop our concepts are a form of programming. Some of our conceptual programming will be self-initiated from our experiences in life and some will be the result of a series of processes or stages that we all go through – rights of passage and all that – though these processes will affect each of us in different ways. The first programming we receive is genetic. It could be said that it is the genetic structure that creates the apparatus of our senses that allows us to process and build concepts and experience percepts. In the sense of this book, we might consider the genes to be the mechanism that created the potential for the attic and its boxes. However, it is the nature of what we put in the boxes and how we deal with things that we experience that creates the 'who' that we conceive our self to be. I know that at this time when we are busy unravelling the human genome that many people are hanging, or attempting to hang, the reason for differing behaviours and physical states on genetic material but that is really only part of a much more complex story that man has yet to discover, which I describe as the other side of the genome – another book I think. If genetic information is the first programming creating our predispositions, the second programming we receive is from our family group. This I term 'familiarisation'.

Familiarisation

The group of people that we are born into is our family. If we are born outside of a family group such as when someone is adopted, there may well be a lack of the fundamental concept of belonging as described in '*What Colour is your Knicker Elastic*'. The family group is composed of a bunch of people that have lived together by a set of familial rules or norms that have been developed over many generations. These rules are long term and set in the never-ending tradition of the ancestors just like the Royal Family. (That is the Buck Palace lot, not the Liverpudlians.) Traditions and rules are the given concepts dictating the behaviour of the family in ways that indicate that we belong to that particular group of people. The drive to adhere to and maintain the familial rules is tied up with the drive to maintain our sense of belonging.

For many, belonging to the familial group maintains their individual sense of security. It is these conceptual rules that make up the essence of what being a 'Smith', a 'Jones' or a 'Longbottom' really is. Smaller isolated nuclear or single parent families who do not benefit from shared familial concepts may need to invent traditions and rules as they go along. This may mean that they are not very stable environments for a child to be brought up in.

As a child in London, I knew and lived with many people whose family line came from the West Indies. One criticism of many the males in these family groups was that they did not take full responsibility for the children they produced. West Indian males were often compared to men of direct African descent who did apparently care for their children. The concept of what a father is in any social or racial groups is subject to tradition passed on from one generation to the next. I talked with as many people as I could and came to the following conclusions as to why there might be this supposed difference.

The people from the West Indies were descended from slaves. Slave traders snatched these people who were put to work in the plantations, for their white masters. When in Africa, I assume that these people had once lived in strong traditional family networks that had been developed over many thousands of generations. When used as slaves, these people were not allowed to live in family units or to develop any natural family structures. The sexes were kept separately and mated at the whim of their owner. Over a few generations, the concepts of any familial traditions, rules or responsibilities had been destroyed. When the concepts of being a father, a husband and a provider have been taken away from people, they no longer see the percept as necessary. Once lost, it can take several generations for that concept to be rebuilt or replaced.

I would not suggest in this that all West Indian men fail to have a paternal concept or that all African men make good fathers, but this example does illustrate a point. Any concept that we hold is generated from somewhere. The source may be internal or external but once the concept is in place it affects all that we perceive. In some cases, the perceptual experience may lead us to reject familial concepts and replace them with the opposite.

Both Marie, my wife, and I came from impoverished backgrounds and we both had fathers who were not good providers. As a conceptual response to what we perceived as children, we have both developed concepts of needing to work hard and be achievers. As a result of that hard work, we live in a large house and have what to many would be seen as a rich life style. Importantly, we both had and continue to have high levels of motivation to work hard. Our children have been brought into a world where most things have been provided for them in a state of comparative luxury. They will either follow our familial concept of hard work and achievement or reject this in favour of low motivation. The jury is still out, as they say. Simon, at thirteen, lacks the motivation to do anything other than fix himself to a computer screen or a television. This may be adolescence or the expression of a generated concept. Kate, at seven, enjoys reading, learning and discovery but it is early days. For Simon, Kate and Josh, twenty-one months, the reality of the concepts they perceive will not be clear until they are in their late teens.

To understand the behaviour of others, we need to know what has happened to them and how their concepts have been shaped, misshaped or destroyed. Whatever our familial group, it is here that our first programming takes place. We develop our first understanding of our self-concept through the shared familial concept and our perception of our part within it. The status that we allow ourselves as adults will often reflect in some way that status allowed us as we developed as children within the family unit.

Social programming

The process by which we learn to relate to the larger group of the society we live in is known as socialisation. Social groups have specific rules and norms. These are very often 'class' based or connected to income level or professional group. Sometimes it is dictated by geographical location. Some parts of a town or the country as a whole are poorer than others. The social niceties and modus operandi will be different in the rough end of Liverpool and the posh end of Henley-on-Thames, likewise in a standard comprehensive and Eton, or a building site and an accountant's office. There may be the sense of needing to be born the right side of the tracks. British society is driven by social and class divide that may be based in working roles or in accents.

Here, I have to admit to changing my own accent from a more East End of London brogue to a Radio Four newscaster. Well, actually it was called the Home Service in those days. I found when I first left home and then left the capital, that outside of London no one would take me seriously with a broad London accent. Those who held the concept that Londoners were not to be trusted perceived me of as a 'fly by night' or a 'wide boy'. With a little practice and a musical ear, I now speak a passable form of BBC, or received English, when I need to, though generally my accent is now probably more a soft southern one. Accents around the country are assumed to have certain social status. Devon and Somerset seem to be seen as strong and thick:

Devon born, Devon bred -
Strong in th'arm and weak in head.

Told to me, would you believe, by a Devonian in a pub, who thought that it was funny? The accent that seems to get the worst press as being 'thick' or 'dim' as in 'not many brains' seems to be Birmingham Black Country. Dundonian has brought telephone help lines, especially complaint lines, to the town of Dundee, as that accent is said to be calming and reassuring. Whatever the social groups we belong to, we have concepts and percepts that we adhere to, and in so doing demonstrate very clearly that we belong or do not belong – either we are one of 'us' or one of 'them'.

Cultural programming

Cultural programming is different from national programming and social programming. Belonging in Britain is not a case of race or colour, it is more about sharing concepts. In Britain, we have many cultures living side-by-side, all of which would see themselves as British. Each culture has its own norms. These rules are fine within the culture, though they may not fit with the country. The rag trade of the 1950s in London was dominated by Jewish immigrants who had settled in Britain but lived in separate, often closed, communities. When a culture lives within yet outside of the host country, it will never be accepted into the social concept. The Jewish settlers in Britain have been absorbed into British society as they have interacted and inter-bred. Being absorbed in this way can be a frightening business for a immigrant culture especially when they have been on the move across the world and have perhaps even been the subject of persecution. When in a host country, cultural identity is a form of security and has the safety of the group. Such security is often tied up with both language and religion. Britain is a mongrel nation that has had genetic input from conquering, immigrating and visiting peoples from all over the world. Perhaps when we can drop into a booth on a street corner and have our DNA analysed while we wait, we will see that being British has nothing to do with race and genetics – it is more to do with shared concepts of what being British is.

In America, following the terrorist activity on September eleventh, Arab, Asian and Islamic groups living in the country who had conceived of themselves as Americans are now getting the message from some sectors of the population that they are perceived as foreigners. The three things that mainly separate us from other groups are colour, accent and religion.

Religious programming

Religious programming is often related to moral programming and the instilling of a sense of rightness and wrongness. Religion generally requires that we adhere to a set of shared concepts. These usually centre on a figure, usually a male, who the followers of the religion agree has some deification and has the ability to communicate directly with, or is in some way a manifestation of, God. These concepts are enshrined in either a verbal tradition where the stories that build the concepts are shared during group meetings or services or may be formally learned in classes as an aspect of a child's education or the conversion of a believer. Those religions that have written texts usually believe these to be in some form the word of God. The priests of the religion will act as interpreters of the text and sometime intermediaries between God and the followers of the religion. All the followers will relate back to the text as examples of fundamental concepts and truths of how we should live, act or be punished. Very often the books relate stories and parables that are designed either to teach a lesson or to give an example of great acts or miracles that have taken place in the name of that religion or deified figure. Most miracles and great acts are recorded in the texts as events that happened historically. Great miracles do not seem to happen in the present. The follower is therefore required to build a conceptual box that holds concepts called beliefs and faith. The stricter faiths are better at programming.

I have to say that the programming received while being educated in Roman Catholic Schools has damaged many of my clients in Britain. Uncompromising zealots in any religion will damage those around them. As religion is generally retrospective, as everything is referred back through the main book of words, it often serves to limit the development of followers. The book is the limiter of forward thinking and change and is the source of the tradition. Because of this fixed thinking or dogma, it can easily be the cause of poverty, disease, over-population and it can limit the social and economic development of an entire nation or religious group. We only have to look as far as Northern Ireland to see the manifestation of two religions both of whom preach forgiveness and love, killing and maiming those that will not accept their concepts.

Religion can often be a sad and dangerous thing. Religion should never be confused with spirituality – they are vastly different and it is possible to have one without the other. As soon as someone believes that it is right to kill in the name of God, we should understand that they have, at that point lost it – this is not spirituality. The kindest things we can do for these people is to inter them in a home for the wretched until they have rearranged the jumble in their attic and developed some better connections. After all, we all need to live or learn to live in peace.

National programming

National programming can be as bad as religious programming. Xenophobia helps no one – least of all the Nation itself. When I was a child, we were told that God is an Englishman, poor old God. As with race, colour and culture, nationality is something to be shared and enjoyed but as soon as we build conceptual boxes that identify us as different from other nationalities, we have become separatist. Once a nation begins to feel superior, we have another master race issue and open the way for another Hitler to take centre stage. Just as with religion, once we start killing other people for the good of the state, we have lost any sense of humanity. For each nation, once a conceptual box has been constructed, all that happens within that box is normal – so that what we do is normal and what you do is strange. When the 'we' refers to national stereotypes, we are really referring to a shared national concept.

British people have concepts of themselves. Usually these hold images like 'bull dogs' and 'Britannia rules the waves' as we set off to reclaim the Falkland Islands. As British, we also have concepts of other races. I can remember my grandfather telling me that he was taught that one Englishman was worth ten Germans, six French and so on. Generally in the British concept, Germans were seen as arrogant, Americans as pushy and show-offs, Italians as cowards, Frenchmen as untrustworthy, French women as sexy – the list of ill-informed and unsubstantiated concepts is endless. When we examine shared concepts of what British people are like, we are told that we are stiff, cold and formal and that British men make lousy lovers – and that can't be true, or can it?

Educational programming

It can be difficult to decide just what education is about. It obviously varies from country to country unless you are British and then it varies from government to government. Very few teachers really understand what the system wants them to do. I decided to have a look at a few dictionary definitions and they add up to something around this.

Education is a process designed to bring up children so that they form acceptable habits, manners, [socialisation] to train them practically and intellectually [to create a useable workforce] and morally [religious education].

Education is probably the greatest killer of creativity that we use to limit the development of our children. Beyond the unwarranted interference by politicians, who are really chasing votes, education is the process by which facts are crammed into the child's mind. Education exists in a form that supports the theories of current experts. These might be experts in the field of education in general or experts in a particular subject. Once we have an accepted authority on any subject, we have placed a limit on development. So that children are not encouraged to have new and creative thoughts and images – they are taught to regurgitate ideas and theories from the past. Even if we were to examine the cutting edge of research and development in any subject – maths, science, psychology, art, any one – we would find that current breakthroughs would take around two years to be published and another three to start to be used in the educational process. It will take another three years for them to become established practice. This means that at best the material we teach our children is around ten years out of date.

Beyond the vote-pulling interference of politicians we must also consider the social engineering that plays a role in directing all education systems. In an industrial age, the requirement of the country is that the young people leaving schools should take up apprenticeships and learn industrial engineering skills. This need for the future workforce dictates much of what will take place during the child's education. The requirements of an agricultural economy or a digital economy will differ greatly and will require a different level of skill development. The education system that we have seeks to impart concepts to our children that are about fulfilling the needs of society as a whole *not the fulfilment of the individual child.*

In the 1960s, the Inner London education authority put a lot of money into supporting the arts and sports in schools. The post war politician seemed to believe that it was time to develop the inner person through the medium of art and the outer person through the media of sport. I note that since the early eighties and Maggie Thatcher's demolition of the teaching profession, that arts and sports are now private activities undertaken by those that can both afford them and recognise their value. The sports field of my youth is now a supermarket and car park. The things that are perceived as important at one time change with both generational and political concepts.

Professional programming

Education does not cease when we leave school. Occupational and vocational training can follow us into our thirties and forties and beyond. As we train into a profession, be it the armed forces, the priesthood, medicine, finance or science, we develop concepts that fit us for the task. Accountants tend not to make good counsellors because they have concentrated on developing logical cognitive concepts and may not be so comfortable with emotional percepts – when people cry, they may not know what to do. Counsellors tend to make lousy accountants for the opposite reasons – when the figures do not add up correctly, they may well cry.

With many managers in British organisations and companies being so bad, I feel sure that the problem is because they have not developed the necessary concepts for the job. They were never trained to do the job. Unless you have the concept you cannot have the percept and many managers simply do not have a clue what they are doing.

In the Health Service, there are managers and chief executives who are psychologists, nurses and doctors, who may all have been absolutely fabulous in their original calling but are, God bless them, absolutely useless as managers. They lack financial, planning and people skills. A trained doctor who is expert in looking up people's bottoms and is skilled in making bottoms work properly, may not be best suited to develop staff support programmes or run a hospital trust. Yet we expect just such people to run our systems and then complain that they do not function efficiently. When managers are unable to do the job, they tend to take it out on those around them. The age old practice known as the 'Peter Principle' of promoting people beyond their abilities often leads to bullying styles of management as inadequate people seek to make up for their own incompetence by shouting at and harassing those that work for them.

Continual programming

Beyond these specific stages of programming, we will each take an individual life path that will continue the programming process. Our relationships, jobs, partners, children, maturation and so on will all contribute to our conceptual make up.

The Happy Baby in the box

At the end of all this conceptual development and programming, is an individual person – you, in fact. There is an inner state recognised by most schools of therapy that would recognise the child within. This is an aspect of our self that we can never lose. If we were a happy, free child, we are able in later life to play, experiment and act spontaneously. If we were a damaged or hurt child, we are cautious, anxious and weary of change. The nature of the child that resides in the conceptual box marked 'inner child' within our unconscious mind will be the result of the conceptualisation and programming that we have undergone. There are many that will say that this is not so and that we are the result of the unchangeable genetic programming that dictates all that we are – that physical stuff that is passed to us from our parents that we are unable to go beyond – as the geneticists say:

Bad blood will out

This assumes that we are slaves to out genes. You can probably guess that I do not subscribe to this theory.

The genetic lobby

I would be a fool and you would probably drag me outside and burn me at a stake if I said that genetic material was unimportant. This would be especially true at the present time when we are unravelling the human genome and making all sorts of connections to states of disease and psycho-social disorders. It is just that I doubt genetics are as important as we now believe. It is the old argument of does the brain give rise to experience or is the brain the result of experience. In short, is this thing we call life generated by the body and the nervous system so that life ceases to be at the point of physical death. Or is there an essential self, spirit, soul or whatever that exists after the point of death that is independent of the physical body? What lies beyond the genes?

The other side of the genome

This and the previous paragraph really do need to be the subject of other books. A pure geneticist would agree with the former idea above and those of a more spiritual bent would agree with the latter. I place myself in the latter camp though I draw a strong distinction between religion and spirituality. All my experience, both personally and clinically, would point to the existence of previous lives and therefore the likelihood of reincarnation. If this is so, then we do not come into this life as clean slates waiting to be written on – a tabla rasa. Instead we are filled to the brim with our own bias and prejudice and what in the east would be termed karmas or samskars.

This experience of previous existence will be having its interaction with our genetic potential and a refining effect on our genetic predispositions. In the debate of whether human consciousness is the result of nature or nurture, I assume that the evolving and reincarnating self interacts with the genetic information so that we may be drawn in certain directions whether they are positive or negative. However, we are still able to exercise choice. The genetic material creates a propensity for us to act in certain ways. It is the exercise of free will that determines what actually takes place. Just because I lack the gene that tells my body to stop eating when I am full it does not follow that I need to become fat. By exercising my free will and consciousness, I can intervene in the process and stop eating because I know intellectually that I have had enough, regardless of what my body and my genetic structure is telling me. I am not being a clever dick. I know that doing or not doing some things can be difficult. Just because something is difficult, that does not mean that I cannot do it.

Those that have a genetic predisposition to consume vast amounts of alcohol or drugs can overcome their habit. Here I note that Alcoholics Anonymous subscribe to the theory that alcoholism is a genetically predisposed illness and prove on a daily basis that it is possible for the conscious will of the person to override the genetic predisposition or habit. The same must be true of genetic gender dysfunctions, paedophilia, kleptomania and so on. We must decide as a race of beings how much of our awareness is genetically based and how much is in our unconscious mind and conscious awareness. Just what do we take responsibility for? I feel another book coming on. The other side of the genome is waiting for us to discover and understand what is there.

6

The Internal Working Map

Columbus discovered America
but you can discover the World.

It might seem strange to say that there exists a map of the universe. I do not mean a map of the physical universe, the stars, planets, galaxies and all. I refer to a map that shows and records the entirety of creation. All that can be touched, seen, smelt, heard, perceived, thought, conceived, intuited, imagined, created, loved and hated. The map does exist; it is all there if we choose to look. Let me show you.

The entirety of creation exists in octaves. This idea is hampered by the connotations of the rainbow and hippy-type responses to the spectrum of colour. Going beyond such prejudice, it is easy to see that all systems have evolved in the same way. The creation of the octave develops through something that is termed the 'harmonic series'. The harmonic series is a natural progression of energy whether the system we examine is engineering, electricity, sound, light, biology, chemistry, psychology, astrology, medicine, whatever – the entire system comes from the same root and evolved in the same way.

This is too short a book to expound such a theory in full, save to say that, once we understand the way the system works, it is possible to make connections between the different disciplines. If we examine a breakthrough that has been made in electromagnetics, the findings can be related directly to the study of human psychology, the building of a bridge or the dissection of organelles in the cell. We need to understand the system. For the sake of simplicity, I will look at the system of sound to explain the development of the harmonic series, relate this to light and then to psychology. Perhaps then we can shed some light on how the material stored in our attic is ordered.

The harmonic series

Whenever there is primary or fundamental wave-motion or vibration, this will set off a series of sub-tones or notes that are known as the harmonic series. The fundamental vibration may be more easily understood by looking at a string on a musical instrument. When plucked or vibrated with a bow, the stretched string goes through a series of motions. The string vibrates as a whole. Let us assume that this note is ‘C’. Simultaneously the string will vibrate in equal parts. The first of these is in half. This adds another sound or tones to the fundamental note being another ‘C’ that is one octave higher than the note that the string is tuned to. The string also vibrates in thirds, fourths, fifths and so on. Each sub-tone that is produced has a ratio to the first note. For those of you with a mathematical bent these are:

2:1, 3:1, 4:1, 5:1, 6:1 and so on.

Simplistically, these harmonics or overtones create a faint echo, in every sound, of what we know as a major scale:

Do Re Mi Fa Sol La Te Do

Or the primary major scale of:

C D E F G A B C

The various body shapes of different instruments will favour different harmonics. So that the same note played on the comparable string will sound different on each instrument, so that a guitar sounds different from a cello or a violin. The balance of these harmonics will create what we hear as good or bad tone – this is something that we might describe as the quality of the sound.

The same principle is true in engineering. It you look at any of the suspended bridges strung over the River Thames in London, the ones with towers and lots of cables, you will see a sign on the pillars at either end of at the entrance to the bridge that requires soldiers to march 'out of step'. This is a throw back to wartime when the streets of London rang to marching boots. The bridges act just like the musical string. The regular footfall of several hundred men can create such a violent harmonic series that the bridge would vibrate itself to pieces. Irregular footfalls create many smaller waves of harmonics that will not damage the structure.

Universal systems

Whatever system we look at, we will find that all forms of energy are subject to the harmonic series and that all natural systems organise themselves in the same way. In the case of optics, a prism will split a beam of light into the natural colour spectrum. In biochemistry, we see the arrangement of the endocrine system. Whether we are looking at the fringes of astrology or the mundanity of the days of the week, we are looking at the same system. In the Ayurvedic personality model, we have the same system as we look at the natural organisation of drives and personality types. For those of a Yogic persuasion, this runs parallel to the Chakra system. In the model that we are using, the natural organisation of the psychology of the person is:

Physical, social, intellectual, emotional, mental, intuitive, creative, fantasy.

Your psycho-harmonics

Just as the note of the single string has all the notes of the harmonic series hidden within it, so do you. Whatever the area or the colour of your fundamental note or personality, the rest of the spectrum is represented by psycho-harmonics within you. Equally, as each musical instrument will emphasise some harmonics and suppress others, each personality does the same thing. When we use the personality model to describe two people as predominantly Blue types they will both be dynamically different because the psycho-harmonics in each will be profoundly different. The structure of your psycho-harmonics is the basis of your individuality. You and your psycho-harmonic structure are unique.

Two part harmonies

When you interact with other people, you will either create a harmony that is pleasant or a disharmony that is not. In the harmonic system, two notes played together create a consonance or a dissonance. A consonance is when the sound is complete. When you hear it you feel that there is nothing else to come. It is the sort of device used at the end of an orchestral piece of music to indicate that it has finished. When a sound is dissonant, it leaves you with the feeling that there is something more to follow to complete or resolve the sound. If a piece of music were to end on a dissonance you would feel left up in the air awaiting the final resolution to complete the sound. Couples are either dissonant or consonant either they are complete or are seeking something else to make it right.

Mapping the unconscious mind

The unconscious mind is no different from any other system and it also complies with the same harmonic principle and organises itself into the same areas as have been shown above. In the model, each drive, state or area is related to a colour

Physical	***Red***	**Mental**	***Blue***
Social	***Orange***	**Intuitive**	***Indigo***
Intellectual	***Yellow***	**Creative**	***Violet***
Emotional	***Green***	**Fantasy**	***Magenta***

Laying out the Attic

The way in which your unconscious minds works is no different from any other system. Your attic will be laid out in areas that are similar to those above. Imagine a large space like the owlery in the tower of Hogwarts Castle in the Harry Potter books. The floor is laid out in sections, each of which is forms a depository for information relating to each of the above areas. Some areas will need to be very large while other may be very small or have nothing stored there at all. Each of these areas is used to store the concepts that make up your sense of who you are and your sense of the world around you. Each of these areas may hold positive or negative concepts and probably a mixture of both. If you find that it is easier to think of your unconscious mind as a cupboard then these areas are the shelves.

Physical concepts – RED

This area in the attic is about your bodily awareness, how you see yourself physically. This may include size, height, weight or, colour. It may be specific and include how you see your nose or breasts, stomach or chest. Your attitude to your body will dictate what you do with it and what you allow others to do with it. It will effect what you eat, how you exercise even down to how you walk, your stance and posture. If you feel good about your body you will have physical confidence. This will dramatically affect what you wear and how much of your body you will let others see. Most importantly, the physical part of our concepts describe how potent we feel, how strong and capable we are to live our lives and face conflict and threat from others.

Red sex

Sexuality as a concept of love is about becoming physically close with another person. To be engaged in the sexual act is as close as you can physically get to another person. The sexual act takes place on many conscious and unconscious levels. The concept of sex that relates to Redness is orgasm. In this sense sexuality and sensuality are different. Both may take place independent of the other, they have no mutual dependence. The concepts you hold about your genitalia and your feeling about how you or others may experience and or enjoy your genitalia, together with your openness to orgasmic pleasure, are all a powerful part of your Red physical concepts in your unconscious mind. For although we, certainly in Britain, are not very good at admitting to or talking about 'it' we are, in reality, all doing 'it' statistically at an average of two and a half times each week. Whether or not we feel that we are being 'done to' in this area or that we are active participants, will depend on the concepts about our sexuality and our sense of worth that we hold in our unconscious mind.

Red fear

The concept of fear is the limiter of whatever area it inhabits. It creates a boundary around our potential progress. Fear at any level will inhibit our development. Physical fear will limit our ability to travel, to attend events and functions to go to places off the beaten track of life. Concepts of sexual fear lead us to hold back perhaps to become fixed in routine and safe behaviours and often to become stuck and fixed. The ultimate concept of Red fear is that of impotence in all its senses.

Social Concepts – ORANGE

This area in the attic is about your sensual and social concepts. Sociability is about liking and being liked. It is a truism that to be liked, we must first like ourselves and in that sense charity does begin at home. Belonging requires clear concepts of what it is I belong to. Once these concepts have been formed, there is the development of what 'us' is. Once I know what 'us' is I begin to have a concept of what 'them' is. Because I have never been 'them' I only have the word of others, hearsay, innuendo, rumour and gossip to guide me. Because of this, the Orange area in the attic will, in all people, be heavy with concepts that are prejudicial. It is too simplistic to say I am not prejudiced, of course I am. I may not have been to Peru but I do have concepts about what it must be like there. I am not female, black, disabled or tall yet I have concepts that prejudge about what it is like to be these things. The distance between prejudicial concepts and fantasy may be very short indeed. In this area, are also the concepts that I hold about my race, nation, country, town, social class, group of friends, workplace, profession, clubs, societies, extended family, immediate family, television, media etc., and how it is that I connect to all of these.

Orange sex

The Orange concept of love is about holding, including and belonging. Sensuality as touching and cuddling is part of a grooming process that leads to concepts of an overall group bonding. In states of intimacy, the concept is that this holding, stroking and cuddling comes to the fore as both fore play and as after play. The orgasm diminishes in importance in favour of the warmth and security of belonging. Sensuality as fore play will often start with a meal, which will also be a sensual experience.

Orange fear

Orange concepts of fear are of not fitting in with the group, being the odd one out, standing out from the crowd. This leads to the development of concepts of needing to maintain group identity through demonstrations such as clothes fashion or hair styling. The conceptual box for the group type has all the ingredients needed to conform. The concepts include the fear of not having whatever it is right to have. Ultimately this leads to the fear of no longer belonging or being seen to belong and therefore being excluded. Social exclusion in that true British sense is known as being sent to Coventry. The ultimate fear is that of total aloneness or isolation.

Intellectual concepts – YELLOW

This area in the attic has two types of concept. The first is something that most people would recognise that concern concepts of 'what it is

I do when I am bored' – it is the concept of 'what do I do when I need a change'. Most of us do something, either regularly or intermittently that is a complete contrast to our everyday life. The second is a constant life style of newness and change. The concepts in this part of the attic are about the analytical dismantling of the existing status quo. The concepts are that 'new' and 'change' are positive and 'existing' and 'traditional' are not. There can also be a sense of fun with a profound need for self-expression.

Yellow sex

The concepts of fun, change and novelty are themes that continue through Yellow sexual and intimate relationships. Concepts of permanence and even responsibility do not belong here. Concepts of the need for variety and change lead to many partners and experimentation.

Yellow fear

Yellow concepts of fear are of being trapped, suppressed or in any way limited. Routine and repetition lead to a monotony of bored acceptance that leads either to the person breaking out in a show of what is seen as uncharacteristic behaviour or undergoing an intellectual death of the soul in which it appears that the person's light has gone out.

Emotional concepts – GREEN

This area of the attic involves concepts of self – with a little 's'. Often these are about how I measure up to other people. This may be a measure of whether I am bigger, better, richer, better looking, more popular, cleverer, more powerful and so on. There is a great need to have recognition as a special individual. Many of the concepts will concern power and most events, issues and items will be seen in terms of the power they might give us. Equally, the concepts will concern what it is that I need as vehicles to give me power. These may include physical violence, social climbing, academic achievements, richness, wealth, and expressions of love, status and position, levels of spiritual awareness or spiritual power struggles in the sense of 'my Guru is better than your Guru', or my ideas, inventions are better than yours or even my scientific breakthrough happened before yours. All concepts are concerned with the exercise of my power.

Green sex

Green concepts of love are big displays of passion. This can be from concepts that noisy is good so that your lover screams and shouts as a demonstration of the size of their love. Or the concept that big and flashy is good leading to huge displays of flowers or very expensive gifts. Anything that is big, loud and showy is seen as good.

Green fear

Green concepts of fear are very much a mirror of the Red. Both have the sense of being powerful and fear losing it. Red physical power has the fear concerned with the concepts of the loss of potency. Green emotional has fear concerned with loss of power wherever the sphere of influence is. The concepts of ultimate loss are around bankruptcy, loss of face, loss of recognition and rejection.

Mental concepts – BLUE

This area of the attic is the natural home of the concept. The concepts of this part of the unconscious mind are actually about boxes. Blue mental process are about internalising conceptual constructs that create a fixed pattern of the external world. The concepts tend towards the ideal and include such concepts as Blueprints for living the perfect life. Many religions, philosophies and psychological theories are held as fixed Blue concepts. Also, the legal system and the law-making bodies such as parliament, the judiciary and the police are upheld as positive concepts of a well-organised and structured society. Paternalistic concepts of authority and fairness are common in this area, including faithfulness, fidelity and fair play.

Blue sex

Often Blue's concepts of love and sex will exclude emotions and often sensuality. This may mean that the concepts are either those of the Red carnal end of the spectrum, or may be a dutiful act born out of concepts such as 'you were never meant to enjoy it' or 'it is a known fact that women do not enjoy sex'. Sex as a dutiful act as the concubine, mistress or loving wife. The sexual act may be part of an arranged marriage to maintain a dynasty or as a brood mare to extend the royal bloodline.

Blue fear

Concepts of fear in the Blue area concern the overturning of the idealistic concepts of order and peace. The two concepts that threaten the Blue area most are Yellow anarchy and general destruction and the Green displays of emotion and power. Many Blue concepts include rules and the laws of parliament are designed to curtail the activities of Yellow and Green.

Intuitive concepts – INDIGO

The concepts held in this area of the attic have gone beyond words and often exists in sound, shapes and colours and a sense of an atmospheric something that cannot quite be grabbed. These concepts concern our deeper feelings about life, the universe, our place in it and the role of people and human destiny. Our sense of God, what happens after death and the ultimate unknowing of intuition and sensitivity. This is the meditative space where concepts of being have greater importance than concepts of doing.

Indigo sex

The concepts in this area are held around the belief that all is love. It would probably be more true to say that Indigo concepts deny the acceptance of hate. The Indigo concept of love is about compassion. Not the passion of the Green, more the compassion of Christ, Krishna or Buddha. Passion can be and often is taken – compassion is given. In intimacy, concepts of love may not include sex despite the fact that couples live together and sleep together. In the extreme, concepts of action are those that only equate to development or resolution of karma, therefore all action should be measured. In some Indigo concepts, thought is seen as the precursor of action, so that to *think* something is as good or bad as *doing* it. Prayer, contemplation and meditation are seen as good thoughts and therefore good acts. The philosophy at work here is the same as that used in absent healing and group meditation. Essentially, to think is to act. Good thought – good act; a bad thought is as bad as the bad action. Thoughts are potentially very dangerous and should be limited and controlled through techniques of meditation practice that take us to the state of meditation where we cease to think altogether, we cease to have a negative effect on the universe.

Indigo fear

Concepts of Indigo fear are based in both Red and Green. Both these areas can show power and energy that is often channelled as manipulation, bullying, aggression, violence and exploitative or perverse sexuality. The concepts of the wrongness of the crudity of these Red and Green areas lead the Indigo mind to seek solace in monastic and meditative pursuits isolated from the rest of the world.

Creative concepts – VIOLET

Creative concepts do not exist beyond words – they both include and exceed them. Concepts of creativity should not be confused with the self-expressive concepts of the Yellow. Yellow concepts of newness are really nothing more than a regurgitation of other people's leftovers. Yellow concepts are forever rebuilding, often in novel forms, the things they have previously destroyed. The first person to use a twelve-bar Blues musical format was creative. The several million that have reused that same musical form have been involved in self-expression. They are expressing their ideas through the creative form of someone else. Violet creativity is the truly original. In most cases Violet creativity is the process of solving problems, though it does include the creative arts.

Violet sex

From the previous books, you will appreciate that Violet is really a balanced state so that it is possible to see the manifestation of all the other colours here in some form or another. However, it would be too simple to say that. Violet concepts of love include all the others actually though are commonly very Red. They are really Red but enacted with some imagination. To take a woman with rough sexual fervour may be a Red concept. To tell a woman that she is the inspiration of the sonnet that you are about to recite to her and then take her with rough sexual fervour is a Violet concept.

Violet fear

The Red concepts of fear are the loss of potency and the Green, the loss of power. The Violet concept of fear is the loss of creativity. To maintain creativity, the Violet type may well put the responsibility onto the concept of inspiration. The concept of an inspirer assumes the power of another person is active in the process. The concept is that without inspiration I have no creativity.

Fantasy concepts – MAGENTA

Fantasies are waking dreams that exist somewhere between the solidity of the Red physical world and the creative imagination of the Violet world. As fantasies, they involve concepts that reject reality. In a fantasy, there are no rules anymore than there is in a dream. For this reason, Magenta concepts have no set form and do not comply with a set of rules – they are free form. This accepts that fantasies can be nightmares as much as fun dreams.

Magenta sex

Dream or nightmare, the fantasy has little to do with reality. Positive concepts of love are sugar and spice and negative concepts of love are hell and damnation.

Magenta fear

This is simply the fear of facing reality. The fantasy normally represents the concept of a safe bubble.

I hope you can begin to get a sense of the different storage areas in the unconscious attic of the mind. Some areas of your attic will be full to bursting while others will hardly be used at all. The problem is that some aspects of the attic become mixed, misfiled and generally messed up. The question is what do we do about it?

7

Who Messed Up My Attic?

A Zebra can never change its spots, can it?

Let us take stock. In boxes stored in our attic, we keep all the factual and structural information that enables us to make sense of the world around us through the use of internal working models and our internal working map. We use this map to subdivide the attic into psychological areas that follow the natural psycho-harmonic series. In this way we use our internal working model or map to develop an understanding of our universe and our place within it. The concepts that we store in the unconscious mind dictate how we see our self, how we see other people and the manner in which we act.

Internal concepts are internal reference points

The concepts that we store in our attic become fixed points or markers that we use to anchor ourselves in a continually changing world. These concepts construct models of how we believe the world is or how we would like it to be. Whether or not these constructed concepts are true or false, positive or negative, we will only know when we put them to the test of reality. I may hold the concepts that people from other races, religion, or sexual orientations are bad, mean or perverted. I will only be able to test these concepts if I go and meet with and communicate with these people in everyday reality. These internal working models are our landmarks, **internal reference points** or IRPs that we use to guide us. These IRPs, however complex, are only a beginning. We do actually test those that we use every day every time we interact with other people or the universe at large. The concepts that we hold in the attic are the starting point from which we venture into the world, the blocks from which we push off at the start of the race of life. This is a race that we start afresh every day.

Parental concepts may never be questioned

If we are lucky, we will have the benevolent support of primary care givers, usually though not always our parents, who impart useful concepts to us. In the beginning, these parent-given IRPs are all that we have to guide and defend us on the journey of life. To create our own individual identity we need to move beyond the concepts of our parents to discover the world for ourself. If this fails to take place, the society that we live in will become static and cease to develop or grow. It is often said that in Britain between the wars there was a static period when things changed very little. When I was a child, people looked back to that time with the warmth of nostalgia. We should assume that if life in stasis is comfortable, there is no need to work for, or develop, concepts of change. It is only when the concepts of the previous generation are challenged and changed that progress or social evolution takes place. The time of questioning the parental concepts is in adolescence. At this time, the concepts are tested and will either be changed or adopted as permanent IRPs, depending on the circumstances and experience of the individual. If concepts were not questioned in this way, we would still be in caves, wrapped in animal skins.

What do you say after you say 'hello'?

We use the IRPs as the basis on which to interact with others. The question of what it is that you say after you have said 'hello' will depend entirely on the contents of your attic. These IRPs are set at an early age. In the analytical school of thought, it is suggested that individuals' gender identity is formed by the time they reach the age of three.

For the boy child, the box that contains all the information about what a man is, how he acts, what is good and what is bad, how he should be seen by others and the appropriateness, or otherwise, of shows of emotion, his sexual identity, behaviour and so on and so forth are all there filed away as IRPs. All the intimate details are there that make up the total image of what a man is or equally what a woman is.

From this information about gender, role and expectation, we begin to create our self-concept, that sense of 'what I am' and 'who am I'. This self-image and self-description will be set from this early age and in many cases will remain fixed throughout the person's life. The longer they persist, it is only with great effort that these images can change or develop. As a rule, the older the person, the more difficult it is to change. Something about old dogs and new tricks, I think. Often great changes will only happen in response to great events. These events are usually catastrophic and involve pain. As we say 'a leopard cannot change its spots'. In reality it can, though I am told that you may need to skin it first. It is often the pain of feeling that we have been skinned that motivates the changes in life.

Apple's don't grow on trees

The other route to great change is not pain; it is that of confusion and the associated loss of identity and sense of self. This occurs in cases where the attic has becomes messed up or jumbled. For the person in this position, there are no IRPs, they may have been lost or are now inaccessible.

> I had a client, Millie, a sedate and dignified lady, who was dipping into the mist of Alzheimer's disease. She would talk to me, for hours if I would let her. Over many months, she made absolute sense until she tilted and, like the Titanic, began to slide into the depths of her unconscious cupboard, out of sight.

As she slipped away, she became progressively more confused. She would often make wild statements that made some kind of disjointed sense to her in her jumbled attic, such as: 'well, a zebra can't change its spots, can it', or 'a stitch in time is better than a bird in the bush'. Her conceptual confusion made a unique set of connections so that boxes describing the ironmongers and the hardware shop became intermingled creating the new profession of 'hard-monger'.

Alzheimer's is a cruel disease. It is as though all the boxes in the attic have been emptied out and their contents mixed so that there ceases to be any coherent internal working model or map of the outside world. There are no longer any IRPs on the inside to explain the outside. All of our perceptual experience becomes very strange and often frightening. The world has become a place where nothing any longer makes any sense. Those people, partners and children who have had intimate involvement become strangers. The boxes containing their information have been moved out of reach so that they can no longer be accessed. In the extreme a box will be emptied so that all the information stored there will have gone – it is simply not there. So the day came when she no longer knew who I was. In some strange way, for me, Millie died that day.

Adolescent attics

For most people, the boxes will also become jumbled during adolescence. The 'who am I' question goes up for grabs at this time as the person plays and experiments with different identities. Many of these identities will scare the parents and that is often what they are intended to do. There is a sense that we, the adolescents, are more in tune and know more than the previous generation who are seen as obsolete, their time passed – we are the future. After all, every generation believes that their time, music, fashion and morals are how it is supposed to be and that the previous generation were weak, insipid and meaningless. Also, we will often look forward with contempt at the next generation feeling that they just do not have a clue, the beat of their music is simply wrong and their fashion peculiar. The adolescent challenges the organisation of the boxes in the collective societal or familial unconscious and suggests alternative patterns and connections that might be better. Every generation does it and in so doing are actually one of the main powers behind the constant movement and drive of human social evolution. Those people currently in positions of power, MPs, teachers, doctors and so on, were children forty, fifty and sixty years ago. For many of these people, their adolescence was spent in or affected by the flower power revolution of the sixties. Many, though they would mostly now choose to deny it, probably smoked dope and experienced free love/sex. They were raised through the Macmillan, post-war

'we've never had it so good'

era, lived through the sixties and seventies

'we've never had it so often'

era, and were challenged about such freethinking through the eighties in the Thatcherian

'sod everyone else and look after your self'

era. Finally the promiscuity and free love was ended by the onset of HIV leading to the

'no one does it anymore'

era, and so the sixties revolution revolved once more. Now peace and love are idealistic fantasies and we can all go off to bomb Afghanistan instead and look out Iraq – Bush has you in his sights.

Concepts of liberalism

Even so, the sixties free-thinking legacy is ever with us. It is hard to see how the Scottish parliament could suggest outlawing the smacking of children had it not been for this social and emotional revolution. When this liberalisation hit its height, the concept of free love it was the changing concepts of sixties adolescents. This was the first time that the previous concepts of emotional, social and sensual restraint had been overtly challenged. Certainly the covert rules that had governed British society since the Victorian era were up for question. The post-war attitude of violence was deemed inappropriate. New concepts of social care, health for all and the power of community were blossoming. There were, and always will be, pockets of entrenched and backward thinking that accept and maintain the more covert Victorian concepts of sexual exploitation and general mistreatment of children and workers. We no longer send children up chimneys or down mines. Although this apparent revolution did not fully overturn the previous order, it certainly redirected it.

The development of the liberal arts of sociology and psychology, counselling and psychotherapy with the related movement towards self-development, describes a general hippification of modern society and government at all levels. How often does a television news broadcast end a story concerning tragedy with phrases like 'the counsellors have been sent in' or 'counsellors have been provided'. Such liberalisation has set us on a course where violent or draconian punishment is unacceptable and the freedom and the rights of the individual are seen as paramount. I note the current government in 2002 are moving with great speed towards legislation for the legalisation of cannabis. 'Far out, man', as they said in the sixties or more accurately, as most of our legislators said in the sixties.

Those clients of mine working the bus and rail services in cities such as Liverpool and London, who are abused, spat at and assaulted on a daily basis by modern adolescents, tell me that the slide into social liberalisation has gone a step too far. 'Bring back the cat'.

Stimulus and response

The bus driver, his passengers, including the adolescents, you and I are all undertaking life's great journey. Once the journey of life has commenced, we are all locked into the eternal law of stimulus and response – known in some areas as the law of Karma and in scientific circles as the law of cause and effect. The everyday results of this law are depicted in Kingsley's Water Babies as 'Mrs Do-as-you-would be-done-by', who ensured that you were treated in exactly the same way that you treated others.

❍ To every action there is an equal and opposite reaction.

We affect the world by everything we think, feel or do. We are always acting as a stimulus and cannot help but affect the world around us. Others interpret every verbal nuance, gesture and facial expression that we have. The mere fact that we are living means that we are a stimulus. Whether we like it or not, we all affect those around us. Those things that we would describe as comprising our enjoyment of life and how we feel will often be the responses from the people and things around us, to us as a stimulus. This is what makes up our experience of the world. If we want to change our experience of the world, we will almost certainly need to change the way we act.

A different stimulus initiates a different response. To explain how and why we experience things the way we do, we have developed theories of luck, fate, chance, predetermination, freewill, religion, politics, science and psychology, acts of God etc. These theories and philosophies are just different ways of ordering the boxes in the unconscious attic so that they begin to make some sort of sense. In the end, whatever model, theory or jargon we use to explain our experience, the bottom line is that we have an effect on the world and the world has an effect on us. We can only know the result of this effect as long as we are aware of how we feel or are feeling about life and are able to take responsibility for our experience. Our experience determines our emotional wellbeing and whether or not our self-image or self-concept is a positive or negative one. The way that we feel about our life, our self, those around us and the situation we find our self in is, in modern psycho-speak, termed our baggage.

Baggage

Baggage is that unresolved emotional stuff that we store in our conscious and/or unconscious mind. Some of it, the conscious bit, we will be aware of though the majority is held below our awareness, as unconscious repressed material. This stuff and its effects are often more visible to others than to ourselves. This would suggest the importance of powerful, open and honest feedback from other people as a tool for self-discovery. Sadly, few people have the guts to ask others for real feedback and are therefore unaware of how they are experienced by others. When feedback is given with love, rather than as a negative form of criticism, it is the greatest gift anyone could possibly offer us. What we see of our own self is like an iceberg – one tenth showing and the rest hidden out of our sight. At the risk of mixing metaphors, let me introduce you to the bergs Emo and Cogni, a nice couple.

Emobergs and Cognibergs

We all know that what we see of an iceberg is the little bit that protrudes above the surface of the sea. It is the unseen nine tenths that make up the bulk of the berg. They are huge, hidden and powerful. The hidden nine tenths of the iceberg can have a devastating effect if approached incorrectly as the Titanic showed all too well. The hidden nature of our emotional and cognitive baggage is similar.

Water in the brain

Imagine, if you will, that your mind is a lake, a deep, still lake. That which is on the surface and just above the surface is the conscious part of your mind. The depth and body of the water is the unconscious part of your mind. On the surface of the water are the ripples of conscious thought, the chatter of everyday life and the constant rat-dropping thoughts of the restless mind. The water in the depth of the lake is altogether different. It is still and dark, meaningful and mysterious. The surface of the water moves quickly as it darts and shimmers in the changing winds and currents of the surface. The water at depth moves slowly and with great weight. This is a much greater body of water whose slow moving currents of the deep sometimes create an undertow that can drag the surface water down – the conscious into the unconscious. That which is on the surface is insubstantial and frothy; it is easily changed and manipulated. The water at depth is much more its own master. When the conscious surface is dragged down, to be confronted by the unconscious, it can have a devastating effect. The conscious mind will only be confronted by the unconscious mind at times of great trauma such as :

- **accidents**, to self or others
- **death**, either unexpected or of someone very close
- **disasters**, flood, earthquakes and so on when beliefs of safety are threatened
- **resonance**, with a present issue such as social workers dealing with child abuse that have unresolved personal issues in the same area may be forced to face their own past
- **pain**, childbirth, torture, abuse
- **drugs**, as all those who experienced 'bad trips' on LSD will verify.

In most cases such confrontations come unbidden and unwanted.

Movements of the mind

One rule of the unconscious mind is that when it moves – in whatever direction – the conscious mind must follow, there is no choice and no stopping it. This is how the stage hypnotist works. When a show is set up, the hypnotist chooses those people in the audience that are suggestible. This means they allow the hypnotists access to their unconscious cupboard and allow him to put things in a box of his choosing. Once the item is in a box, in the form of a post-hypnotic suggestion, it becomes a part of the person's inner concepts concerning who they are. Once inside a box, it will be played out by the conscious mind. However, the conscious mind will have no awareness of why it is being played out because the unconscious mind is below our awareness. The person has no understanding of why they are doing what they are doing.

This is the reality of Jung's teaching of unconscious material being something that is inside us yet beyond our control. If, while in hypnosis, subjects are told that they will perform an act when the hypnosis comes to an end, they will have no choice other than to allow that suggestion to play itself out. So, if a given post-hypnotic trigger is put in the box, perhaps a double rap on the table, when I hear it, I connect to the box in my unconscious mind and find the concept that this trigger is connected to is one of me opening a window. I get up and open the window. My conscious mind will observe me doing this but not understand why. If questioned, the conscious mind will search for a reason to justify such an action. This means that the conscious mind will sift through the boxes in the unconscious in an attempt to understand. In reality, the conscious mind will light on a concept that it finds plausible. The conscious mind is asking the unconscious, 'why would I open a window?' I might find concepts such as, 'I experienced the room was stuffy' or 'I was feeling that it was too hot in the room'. The truth is I did what I did because I had no choice.

❍ **Unconscious material must be played out by the conscious mind.**

Justification and rationalisation

Makes you wonder about the man who maintains he is an animal lover yet, when he goes home, he kicks the cat. I always find it a hoot when I meet someone who is an animal lover but eats meat or the vegetarian who is wearing leather shoes. When we point out to someone that there is discrepancy between the person's behaviour and their proclaimed beliefs, they will attempt to make up for this shortfall by justifying or rationalising what they have done. When we hear ourselves justifying and rationalising, we are really saying that there is a mismatch between what we say and what we do. That takes me back to the, 'don't do what I do, do what I tell you' attitude of my parents.

Successful advertising is a form of hypnosis

The successful advertiser has just that hypnotic effect in developing brand loyalty. I will continue to play out the suggestion that the advertising has slipped into one of my conceptual boxes. If I am questioned, I will rationalise and justify my purchases in a way that makes sense to my conscious mind. The stage hypnotist however, is slightly different from the advertiser in that the subject in hypnosis is affected for the period of the act. Advertising is an ongoing process of feeding in concepts that will build on brand loyalty. Also, the effects of the stage hypnotists are dramatic and immediate. In the stage show, we find the fat roly-poly man acting out the part of a gazelle as though he were a natural ballet dancer – he has no choice other than to play out the contents of the post-hypnotic suggestion implanted in the 'who am I' box – 'I am a ballet dancer'. Advertisers seek to drip feed their message. Kellogg's need to advertise corn flakes is to maintain their market share not to increase it – their approach is a continual drip-feed to keep us loyal.

Stage hypnotism, as opposed to clinical hypnotherapy, conducted as a show, is only possible with around one in thirty of the audience who are termed 'Somnambulists'. These people have loose lids to their boxes and are subsequently easily suggestible and often gullible. Those amongst us who are not somnambulists either have tighter fitting lids or have an attic which is organised in such a way that rational boxes filter information as it enters and leaves the attic. This makes us not so gullible. Though, if the filter is a little too strong we lean toward the sceptical and have problems letting any new ideas in or letting our emotions out. This can make us appear, or actually be, fixed and unchangeable.

Healing-hypnotherapy

The hypnotherapist in the consulting room is seeking to heal. You do not need to be a somnambulist to benefit from hypnotherapy. Anyone can be hypnotised and benefit from it. In terms of susceptibility to being hypnotically induced, it can be more difficult to work with those people who have loose lids to their boxes and are somnambulists because as much as you try to put stuff in the boxes, it can so easily fall out again. The post-hypnotic suggestions added to boxes during hypnotherapy are used to modify thought processes and associations of feeling and patterns of behaviour by adapting or altering our inner reference points.

The skilled analytical hypnotherapist can go beyond that of adding to the contents of a box with post-hypnotic suggestions to the removal of unwanted material from a box by using specialised analytical interventions. In some case, the boxes in the attic can be removed or generally reordered or reorganised, internal working models can be rebuilt or repaired and internal working maps redrawn. It is true that all forms of psychotherapy can do similar things. It is just that good effective hypnotherapy allows more direct access to the unconscious mind, whereas the work of other therapies is moderated and filtered through the conscious mind, which slows things down considerably. Conscious therapeutic work almost always takes longer than unconscious therapeutic work. Because of this difference of approach and technique, traditional analysis as a talking therapy may take a protracted time of three to five sessions a week for up to five years, as opposed to hypno-analysis which at one session per week may take one to three months to have a similar effect.

Forms of hypnotherapy

Suggestive hypnotherapy involves adding material to boxes. Analytical hypnotherapy seeks to reorder boxes and tidy up attics. Analytical hypnotherapy has a lasting effect. If forms of suggestive hypnotherapy are used, the effects of the post-hypnotic suggestions are sometimes short-lived. Suggestive smoking cessation therapy may be very effective in the short term but the effects of the post-hypnotic suggestion will be gone after a few months and the person who stopped smoking so easily is now smoking again. Analytical techniques seek to sort out why there is a need to smoke in the first place. This identifies the particular problem as a cause and the act of smoking as a symptom of that cause. If the problem is solved so that the cause is no more, the symptom of smoking simply disappears, we no longer need to do it.

Waking hypnosis

Of course, we do not need to be in a continual state of hypnosis to take on post hypnotic suggestions. The sharing of propaganda, general information and advertising are all doing exactly that. Some of us are more susceptible than others. When a person's boxes are easily opened it can seem as though they have no mind of their own. Have you ever met the type of person who is so suggestible that their point of view is coloured by the opinions of the last person they talked to. These people are a continual frustration to partners and friends because they are forever changing their point of view. They are a dream for advertisers and sales people, who require the short-term loyalty of the quick sell.

Back to the bergs

Emo-bergs then are composed of the one tenth of our **feelings** that we are aware of in the conscious mind and the nine tenths that we are unaware of in the unconscious mind. **Cogni-bergs** are the one tenth of our **thoughts** that we are aware of and the nine tenths that we are not. The unconscious part of our self, by far the larger part, has a fundamental effect on the conscious part of our self. We can only understand why we feel, think and act they way we do if we take some time to unpack the boxes, cupboards and attics of the unconscious and understand what is going on below the surface. This is normally the result of psychotherapy or self-development which is self-psychotherapy. The motivation that takes us to the point of therapy will vary. As I have stated in other books, the energy that leads us to make the choice to change our life is either the insight that happens when we have realised that changing our self is timely and appropriate, or as most of us do, change occurs in response to cognitive, emotional or physical pain. This is when it becomes too painful to remain the way we are. Change at all levels in thinking, feeling or doing occurs either through the process of pain or that of awareness. Change through awareness is conscious change. Change through pain is unconscious change that may be forced into conscious awareness.

Why store material?

The question of why we get involved in all this storing business needs to be addressed. It really would all be rather simpler if we dealt with issues as and when they occurred. So why don't we? In the case of the attic, we need to store up concepts to help us make sense of our experience. But why store negative material in the cellar? The initial answer to this question is that no one knows. Well, that is to say that I have spent my life attempting to find someone that does know and I have failed so far. There are some theories though and the bottom line seems to be that we repress, or store in the unconscious cellar issues and items that we feel unable to deal with at the time.

The majority of repression seems to take place in childhood and the tendency to continue doing this fades through the teenage years. The mechanism seems only to be reactivated at times of extreme fear or pain. In the road traffic accident, we do not remember going through the windscreen of the car. One minute we are driving, the next we are in the road or hospital. The painful, fearful bits are lost or repressed in the unconscious mind. We do not see the glass shatter; feel it cut our face or the bone of our skull snap.

The same is true of childbirth. I am sure that if women did not repress the pain encountered during labour they would only ever do it once. They seem to be able to pack it away in a box that they seem to be unable to reopen until the same thing is happening again – the labour has started, then they begin to remember all too clearly. Then they get off the bed and head for the door saying, 'I don't actually want to do this just now'.

In the main, repressed material is boxed in early and formative years. This is why the psychiatrist and psychotherapist will want to know about the patient's relationship with their father, mother, siblings and so on. Take a trip around those early years, fears and excitements. Most psychotherapies start with a version of 'this is your life'. The 'how was it for you' question. That really takes me back to the point where I came into the book – Eileen the mother I almost had.

My mother hiding behind my father

In my conscious awareness, the inner box labelled 'mother' was filled with positive and warm feelings. They concerned a woman who I saw as consistently mistreated by a bullying man, her husband and possibly my father. I have a box in my unconscious mind labelled 'Father'. I was twenty-five years old when I first made serious attempts at opening the box as I endeavoured to deal with the effects of the contents. I went into formal therapy. I had previously been to mediums, quacks and priests and had chance encounters with people who claimed to help others untie the knots in their heads but now I needed something more, something that would work for me. Something that was formal and contracted with set goals. My aim, or so I thought was to resolve many and various bits of baggage I was carrying concerning my father. He had been an abusive parent whose behaviour towards me led me to leave home at the age of fifteen.

I stated as much when I first met my therapist, a lady named June. It took several attempts to find a combination that would allow an entrance into my unconscious stores. Having discovered the entrance, June encouraged me to journey within and after a while we found the box marked 'Father'. It seemed to be hiding on a shelf in the darker recesses of my inner cupboard in the blackness of my cellar, not in the bright light of my attic. The cellar is a place that I do not visit unless I have to. Going with June to that place inside me was painful and I had spent my life avoiding it. Somehow in the holding environment of June's consulting room and June's strength, I was able to begin to unpack the box with her in the safety of this newfound therapeutic bond. Once found, it had taken me several more sessions to prize the box open and several more before I could begin to examine the contents. Pain and fear can be an inhibiting factor. Finally, we developed a rhythm that allowed a useful though not overpowering movement forward. In one session, to my great surprise, out of a connected box came pouring a torrent of negative emotion related to my mother. It was as though it had all jumped up and bitten me when I was least expecting it. Now I had to open examine and reorder the 'mother' box.

My mother unwrapped

In my mind, my memory, my heart and my head I was angry with my father for how he treated me. Angry for how he had treated my brother and sisters. Especially angry for how badly he had treated my mother. In the conscious part of my mind, my mother was a goddess. She was an angel who was oppressed and despoiled by this devil figure of my father.

I recalled times when I had looked at my mother at fêtes and village halls comparing her with the mothers of my friends. In some Oedipal fixation, I had seen her with total love. But now, what was this. My unconscious mind was tearing apart these positive feelings. These images now appeared false. Not in the sense that they had not happened but in the sense that there were other darker images that told of another story. A kaleidoscope of fractured images repeated themselves in circles in my mind. The forgotten times when she also hit us. The beatings in the kitchen with the clothes brush. My mother hitting me harder and harder because I refused to cry, us locked in a battle of wills and she breathing heavily, exhausted and making noises that I now know to be like those of a woman wrestling with her body and mind, desperately forcing herself to come to orgasm.

Not the only time when I have felt the close interconnection of violence and sex all wrapped in the package of abuse. Though that was not it. There was something else in the box that seemed to elude me. I knew that whatever my mother did, it was nothing compared to those things done by my father when the mood was on him. Then it all fell out. In the rush of emotion that swamped me, I realised that my mother had never stopped my father's behaviour towards me.

From somewhere deep inside me came unresolved feelings of abandonment and anger related to my mother. It was as though I had been attacked, mugged, jumped from behind. I just did not see it coming. It took me completely by surprise and left me in a state of shock. Many sessions were used as I began to reconstruct my supposed experience of past events. My mother let me down. She abandoned me to my father. She did nothing to save me, to save any of us. The little boy within me cried with the pain of abandonment.

It is the conscious part of our memory that is the tip of a much larger body of repression that inhabits the darker recesses of our unconscious mind. In this case my father is really the tip. It is my mother who has been submerged in the depth. There was a very definitely a 'father' box that needed attention. The father box with the unresolved issues was hiding those relating to my mother. It is just such things that make up the contents of our cupboards. The tip that we are aware of in our conscious reality is a bit part player in a much greater drama.

The contents of a box my not be true

The mind can play tricks and the images that we see and the memories that we recall may not be altogether true, as they may not contain the whole picture or the whole story. The mind is a partial organ. Often when I am working through deep issues with clients, the issues and images that they raise may seem a long way out of line, so that they ask me if what they are remembering is actually what happened or are they making it up. This is particularly true of childhood abuse issues. My response is that what they experience is the product of their unconscious mind. If the images they see are not real, there is actually a reason why the unconscious mind has produced them. If the image in a dream is that of being raped by a known or unknown figure, it may be that the client feels that they have been violated emotionally or mentally by this figure. It may not have actually been sexual abuse. It may be that the unconscious is expressing inner feeling using these images as metaphors. Such things can create great controversy as in what had been termed false memory syndrome.

When I was four years old, I opened the kitchen door to see my father, who was standing by the gas cooker, backhand my eldest sister with what was known affectionately as a 'fourpenny one'. From the force of the blow, she flew across the room and hit her head on the opposite wall. Stunned, she slid down to the floor, her glasses at a comical angle and her skirt around her waist showing her knickers, just like a cartoon character. I knew when it was best not to be in the presence of my father and ran at full pelt up the stairs to my bedroom where I hid, crying and shaking under the bed until I was sure the coast was clear.

This was one the first items to come out of my box marked 'Father' and my first example to myself to justify my feelings of what a horrible man he was. Many years later, when I was talking with my eldest sister, I discovered that on the day in question, she had been helping my mother do some cooking. They had a pan of water boiling on the stove awaiting some eggs. In the operation of putting the eggs in, my sister has pulled the pan of boiling water towards herself. The act that I had seen as continued abuse by my father was really, as a rarity, him acting for the benefit of others and attempting to save my sister from first-degree burns or scalds. This event had been included in my sister's box marked 'father' as evidence that he was really not so bad after all.

There may be several agencies that mess up the attic. We can be sure that this will only happen at times when we are impressionable. It can be that some of us are always impressionable but for most of us it will be at the point of pain, shock or horror. Or it may be when we are emotionally vulnerable such as when we fall in love. Then we are only safe if the person we fall in love with feels the same way and treats us with care and respect. However, we must accept that we all have a few loose lids here and there. At some time, we will all be susceptible to advertising and propaganda, declarations of love, gossip and prejudice. We are human after all.

Loose lids in business

Most organisations have things that they would rather hide. Things that have been hushed up, covered up or have been got away with. Boxes and their contents need to be kept shut. Eventually, many of these shut boxes burst open with devastating effects on the staff, customers and shareholders, as, for example, when the apparently respectable Enron and World.com were shown to be rotten and cancered to the core.

The reality that many of business's household names were built on the slave trade, gun running or opium is something that we do not attend to. There are also secrets that need to be kept hidden. These may be industrial secrets and processes, ingredients and ideas. Industrial espionage is a real thing. The first person to the market place makes the money. Just as advertisers seek to put things in boxes and hypno-analysts seek to take things out, spies in business and politics are doing the same thing. They may want something or want someone to do something. They may also use pain as their preferred tool of change – honey-traps, blackmail, fear and bribery are all useful tools in gaining or changing concepts and controlling behaviour.

8

Keeping the Cupboard Shut

There's rats in the cellar.

Up to this point, we have looked at the programming of concepts in the attic of the unconscious mind. What we have been examining are the psychological processes that take us from birth and through our learned experience to equip us with our sense of our self and our sense of the world around us. These we will term '**the structural concepts**' as they are the building blocks of our perception. These are the things that we develop through our programming as internal reference points (IRPs) that guide us through life. At times of pain we will modify these, sometimes dramatically. Also through the process of maturation, we will slowly modify some attitudes and will, in the main, feel less anxious about life and generally mellow, as we get older.

The place that we keep all the material that we do not want to look at or go anywhere near is the cellar. Cellars are dark, damp places accessed by a set of rickety or unfriendly stairs. The light usually does not work and the only access to the outside world, other than the rickety stairs, is the coal-shute. It smells musty down here and cobwebs hang from the flaky-paint ceiling. The material that we keep in the cellar is the result of interactions based on the material we keep in the attic. It is as though the attic is the theory, and very often the ideal. The cellar is the reality of our experience of how life actually is. We will term these '**the reality concepts**'.

Many of our structural concepts will never be tested. Remember, we may all know that Peru exists without actually going to check that it is there. However, we will only be able to test the structural concept that we hold in the attic in the box marked 'Peru', if we actually go there and experience it. I can remember people on the council estate that I grew up in who believed that the Vietnam war did not actually happen and that it was all filmed on location. The same was true with the moon landings that some people were convinced never took place but were filmed in a studio. The result of putting the structural concepts into effect creates reality concepts. When we develop reality concepts without testing the structural concepts, we are engaging in prejudice and possibly fantasy. Prejudice is when we make the assumption that what we hold in the attic is true without putting it to the test – we then process this non-experience into a reality concept and store it in our cellar.

What do we store in the cellar?

Reality concepts come in two varieties. Those that confirm our structural concepts or require us to make slight alterations to them. These reinforce our structural concepts and increase our sense of security because we are sure that we know where we are in a changing world – we are safe. Then there are those that are so different from our structural concept that we cannot face them. They require us to adjust, change or create new structural concepts, often about difficult issues that we reject. Sometimes the issues involved just cannot be faced. The reality concepts that we find hardest to deal with will be stored in the back of the cellar.

When Mary married Peter, her structural concept about marital sexuality involved soft and sensual warm intimacy. Indeed that had been the way that it had seemed during the time that Peter courted her. There had been times when he was a little rough. Mary made sense of any roughness by referring to the box in her attic labelled 'passion' and paid some attention to the one labelled 'lust' and another labelled 'enthusiasm'. After the marriage – actually while they were on their honeymoon – the whole tenor of their sexual interaction began to change. Peter wanted, well actually demanded, that she start to engage in acts that bore no relationship to her structural concepts of soft and sensual warm intimacy. These were actually painful and also degrading to her. When she voiced her feelings, Peter hit her. He hit her where it would not show. It did not show and no one noticed.

These experiences, reality concepts, were for Mary so far outside of her ideals and expectations, her structural concepts, of what she felt that she ought to be feeling and experiencing, that she took that path commonly taken by the abused and tortured – she became numb to all that was taking place. At night, her living hell became a misted space that was simply endured. Over the years in that dark space she did things that by now included appliances and on occasions other people. All these things were outside her ideal structural concepts. During the days, she was her normal sparkling self. No one knew, not even her mother or her best friend. It was only when she was fifty-five years of age when Peter, at sixty-five years of age, died of a heart attack, that she began to address the hidden aspects of her life. It was then in a counselling session, ostensibly about her bereavement, that her story about the years of abuse she had suffered tumbled out of her cupboard.

Peter and his violence had established a locking mechanism that kept Mary's cellar door firmly closed. Whilst more and more stuff went in, she was unable to allow any stuff to come out. To this day, her family and friends all believe that Peter was a good chap and that he and Mary had the perfect relationship.

When we come across someone who continues to put up with a situation that is deeply negative for them we often wonder why on earth they would choose to stay in it. This is really our own prejudicial concept coming into play. When people find that the discrepancy between the structural concept and the reality concept is too great for them to face up to, so difficult that they are unable to justify or rationalise it even to themselves, they will go into denial. They will push all the unprocessable material in the cupboard and bang the door shut. Each time there is an issue to deal with, they will do the same thing. This is great short-term strategy to cope with a difficult situation that may work for years. If it develops into becoming a way if life, in the end the cupboard will be full to bursting. As the doors creak, the person begins to feel anxious and worried, sleep patterns begin to break down and panic attacks may develop. Somehow, he or she must keep the cupboard doors shut. The fear of the contents spilling out and being faced or becoming public may lead the person to do anything possible to keep the doors firmly shut. The locks that we use will depend on the type of person that we are.

The locks that keep the cupboard shut

All locks are a form of displacement activity. This is when the energy and resources that should be used for solving a problem are redirected so as to take the conscious focus away from the problem. This is burying one's head in the sand, the ultimate avoidance.

Mary used the lock of denial to keep her cupboard doors tightly shut. In short she pretended to herself and everyone else that it was not happening. Actually she had two locks, one was denial and the other was the fear of how much Peter might hurt her if she faced up to what was happening and did something about it. Cupboards and cellars have many different types of lock. Denial is probably the most common lock – just pretend that nothing is taking place. Denial is like having an anaesthetic – it just all goes away. Many locks have a numbing effect actually caused by anaesthetics such as alcohol or drugs, prescribed or otherwise. If we return to the Ayurvedic personality model, we can begin to get an idea of how different personality types avoid opening cupboards. For many, the lock of denial would be termed as using the magenta part of their personality to avoid reality and build an internal fantasy.

What's your poison?

Keeping the door securely shut is related to the part of the person that we would describe as security. When people feel secure and safe, they are at ease and happy. The purpose of the cupboard and the cellar is to hide away any material that might threaten our sense of security. The methods we adopt in our attempts to keep the door shut will therefore depend on what we see as giving us security. The following should give some indication of how differing personalities approach the concept of locks. Remember from the previous books that each drive is composed of varying aspects of the three basic components of Thinking, Feeling and Doing. It is the subtle blending of these three components that make up the eight personality archetypes.

Red physical locks

Red personalities are dominated by the physical need to be doing something. This leads us to the immediate understanding that for this person, both thinking and feeling are not comfortable qualities to deal in. This suggests that the Red cellar is probably full of unresolved thoughts and feelings that been avoided by doing something else instead. The Red lock is often seen as displacement activity, avoiding facing the difficult issue by doing something else instead. All types of personalities use displacement to avoid dealing with difficult issues but Red types are masters in the craft, as are yellow types.

Ged and Kate have been married for eight years. Kate, learning not to make emotional demands of Ged, has maintained the relationship. For Ged's part he has always gone and 'done' something else whenever difficult issues have arisen. As a Red type of person, the doing something makes sense for him. His inner thoughts and feelings unsettle him, so, in the main, he ignores them. They had come to therapy because Ged had an affair. The affair had been Red physical displacement after he and Kate had an argument about the amount of time he spent out of the family with his 'mates'.

It became apparent during the sessions that this physical act was a displacement of Ged's need to tell Kate how angry he felt about what she had said. The sexual act with a stranger was explicit. He did not come home from a night out and when he arrived the next morning, he

> smelt of an unknown perfume. The affair had happened three months ago and Ged has been unable to discuss his feelings despite continual efforts from Kate to get it all out in the open. It was only when Kate communicated in a physical way – she threatened to leave him – that he agreed to come to counselling. The process of counselling was very difficult for him as it involved him looking at his feelings and explaining his thoughts, both currencies that were difficult for him. His comment to Kate after a difficult session was that all this talking was a waste of time and that if she would let him have sex with her again, everything would be all right again.

For Ged, physical activity or doing something is his 'Lock'. It is the way he uses his energy to avoid difficult situations and to take his conscious mind away from the need to look in his cupboard. He has lived a life in which he has avoided the emotionality of his relationship with Kate by going out with the 'boys'. He used the physical/sexual affair as a bargaining tool and a form of punishment to Kate – he assumed that the physical act of sex with Kate would work as means of bringing about or affirming a resolution.

When the doors of the Red cellar are bursting open, the lock that will be applied will almost always be a physical doing lock. In crude terms, this may be seen as fight or flight, either hit it or run away, making it very difficult for Red people or those involved with Red people to resolve conflict. It can simply be just too difficult to talk about the problem and the idea of showing feelings or emotions is completely out of the question.

Orange social locks

The orange world is dominated by feeling. For this person, both thinking and feeling can be a problem. Another way of looking at the thinking process that leads to action would be to call it taking responsibility. Orange people do not want to take responsibility. Therefore the initial lock employed is to give the responsibility to someone else. This is the 'them' as in 'it is their fault'. So the Nazis can blame the Jews and society can follow in an emotional blindness without thinking about what they are doing.

Come to think about it, we might draw the same parallel about how the Israelis are treating the Palestinians. Blind action against 'them' without thinking about or talking about what we are doing and the consequences, can only lead to disaster. The other side of the orange lock is to assume that someone else will make it alright: 'they will never let it happen, will they?' People that do not want to think or be made to act will avoid conflict. The most common lock is pretending that something does not exist. 'If we do not pay attention to it, it does not exist'.

Betty and Jack live in a London suburb – she is a housewife he is a butcher. Their daughter Janet had brought home her boyfriend Simon. Jack and Betty live an orange life that seeks to avoid conflict within the family house. They like to feel cosy and safe and dislike the uncomfortable feeling of someone rocking the boat. Janet knows the rules, as she has been brought up in them and has been playing them for many years. Simon is an intellectual and questions the things he sees around him. Simon makes Jack and Betty feel a little uneasy. They are drinking tea and watching the television sit-com 'Till Death Us Do Part'. This is a prejudicial little programme where much humour is made of the main character, Alf Garnett, being racist, sexist, chauvinistic and xenophobic. Simon is moved to anger by some of the jokes and says so. 'This programme is a disgrace – surely he can't get away with saying that – he is a sexist pig. How can you watch it?' Bet leans across Janet and puts her hand on Simon's knee. 'Simon dear, in this house we have one rule. We do not discuss sex, religion or politics. Okay?'

This is an interesting situation. The television programme is full of all the things that cannot be discussed in the house – sex, religion and politics. However, Bet and Jack do not need to make any decision about whether or not they should watch it because 'they' – the BBC – have put it on the screen. In work, 'they', the work colleagues, say things like, 'that Alf Garnett, he is so funny'. Bet and Jack can laugh at the jokes and allow the programme into their home on the basis that they do not have take any responsibility for it or for their enjoyment of it. In the same way, many people have stood back and watched other people being assaulted, beaten, murdered, hanged, guillotined and whipped because 'it was nothing to do with me'. Not taking responsibility for who you are or what you are is a powerful lock.

Yellow intellectual locks

Yellow is the natural home of the displacer. Whereas red displacement is to do something, yellow displacement is about avoiding doing something. Yellow types tend towards procrastination and will often do anything to avoid the need to act or face things, especially emotional issues. Yellow personalities are thinkers, which means that they have problems with feeling and doing. Feeling in this case means emotional commitment, so they exhibit problems with being committed to any course of action for any period of time. This is the person who is so fearful of commitment that when you ask, 'do you love me?' can only manage to say, 'I really like you a lot'. The natural lock for them to avoid commitment is to change, move on – it is time to get out of it. To stay too long involves facing up to and understanding emotion and emotions are to be avoided.

Ben is a demolition expert. Not of buildings or walls. He demolishes people and situations. He likes to take things apart to check how they work but he is not too hot at putting them back together. He has emotions but he views rather as an observer, a scientist or researcher. In his observation, he is not actually connected to his own feelings. Several times in his life he has attempted to contact his emotions. His initial attempts with women became problematic. The emotions of the women became involved as well which clouded the issue so that Ben lost his understanding of his own feelings and began to feel that he was being swamped by emotions and demands. Whenever this happened, Ben packed his bag and moved on. He failed to understand why the women became so angry with him. He was

> perfectly capable of rationalising and justifying his actions, though, to the women, his explanations seemed to make no sense at all.
>
> His emotional experience began to develop as a rush of excitement whenever he encountered something new. He enjoyed this sensation, which led him to seek out more and more new experiences. This seemed to Ben a good trade-off. If the situation he was in became too difficult to handle, he would move on. Moving on has become the lock that keeps the doors of his unconscious cellar firmly shut. Emotional issues are simply not addressed. This is not immediately apparent to his potential partners who experience him as engaging, interested and concerned. It is only when they attempt to contact his real feelings that they hit the lock as he withdraws and justifies his departure.
>
> Ben has found a safe way of experiencing a thrill of emotion through the medium of fear. It started when he jumped from a plane on his first free-fall jump. The experience was so intense that it made him cry. At twenty-eight years of age, these were the first tears he had shed since the age of ten.

This really does illustrate how one man's ceiling is another man's floor. The things that you do that you might find exhilarating, things that put you in touch with your emotions, might scare the living daylights out of me. Ben is able to use the emotion he experiences through dangerous situations as a means of locking the cellar doors that hide his real, unresolved feelings. In the world of rationalisation and justification, he is able to convince himself that he is an emotional person. In my world, that can be quite intensely emotional. Ben's experience is to me cheap emotion, contrived emotion, thin and diluted. Yet for Ben, the intensity of my emotions would be seen as swamping, irrational and over the top. But I do other things to keep my cellar doors shut.

Green emotional locks

Green personalities are a paradox of opposites. As we review this green personality, just remember this. Green types are loud and egotistical because they feel small and insignificant – they seek power because they feel impotent. Green comprises large amounts of feeling and doing. They are deficient in thinking. This can, and often does lead to a personality type who acts like a headless chicken running around to no purpose. High levels of emotional commitment to action are the ingredients of a powerful personality. However, unless this potential for power becomes directed, it simply escapes into free space as hot air, irrational outbursts and bluster. Green locks are used to avoid facing cellar contents of fear – fear of being seen as small or insignificant or the fear of loss – of position, status, recognition, power, possession, other people. A very common lock for the green to avoid facing difficult issues in the cellar is shopping. Retail therapy is what your flexible friend is for. Many Green personalities will surround themselves with possessions and shows of wealth and power. The most common lock would be summed-up as 'attack is the best form of defence'.

Joan is an auxiliary nurse in an NHS Trust. She works on ward 47 and has been there the longest of all the staff. Over twenty-five years, she has seen sisters and nurses come and go. She has seen the changes in the system as various governments have come and gone trying out their new ideas. The one constant thing on ward 47 is Joan. Joan knows this and feels that she in someway owns the ward. She has communicated this to the hospital at large and the hospital at large seems to have accepted this. No one thinks about ward 47 without thinking about Joan – Joan's feelings are taken into account. All the team including the ward sister defer to Joan for one reason, they are scared of her.

Joan is Green. She is possessive of her ward and her position and she is prepared to fight for it. This has never come to physical contact though it has come close. Her main form of attack is her emotional outbursts. If you upset Joan, you know about it along with the rest of the hospital. Joan, unlike most British people, is emotionally open and prepared to confront anyone. Anyone seeking to change her routines or the ward systems takes their life in their hands. If anyone criticises her, her defence is attack and she screams and shouts, becomes emotionally volatile and is threatening. People therefore avoid confronting her and Joan keeps her cellar door firmly shut.

Emotional personalities will always have problems in rationalising their feelings. Analysing why they act in a certain way is not easy for them. When questioned, they can be left feeling vulnerable or small. The smaller they feel, the more extreme the reaction. It does not matter if they are the cleaner or the managing director, the power of their response will be directly proportionate to the smallness that they feel. The fear of loss can be dominant so that they may be motivated to gather great fortunes and acquisitions so that, come what may, they are safe. When currencies are under threat, we are told that people invest in gold. It is really the threatened green types who are out buying the ingots.

Blue logical locks

Blue personalities are dominated by thinking and doing. Their area of weakness is feeling. This creates an energetic logical person who is often devoid of emotions, an idealistic and dutiful person who will tend to do 'what is right'. This is actually an avoidance of emotions. Doing what is right is following a system or blueprint. The blueprint for living is required because emotions are things that are seen as uncertain and difficult to deal with. The difficulty is bound up in the fact that feeling cannot be weighed, measured or logically quantified. Blue types fear emotion and have locked so much of their own emotions away that they resort to logical thinking as a lock to the cellar doors. The Blue man is the one who is so far removed from his emotions that his response to the passionate question, 'do you love me?' is to think, 'well, I married you didn't I'? This lack of emotional empathy and understanding leads to a personality type who is often fixed, stubborn and immoveable. The most common lock is to use logic to avoid facing emotion.

Joseph is a good logical Blue type. He has been married to Anne for twenty-eight years. Together, Anne and Joseph are waving goodbye to their third and last daughter who is driving off for her first year at university. Anne goes into the kitchen to make a cup of tea and is surprised to see Joseph in the doorway with a suitcase. He has come to tell Anne that he has been having an affair for the last eighteen years and that he has stayed with her to fulfil his duty as a father. He had always promised himself that he would stay until the last child had left home and now he was leaving. Joseph is so disconnected from his own emotions – they are locked firmly away – that he cannot understand why Anne did not thank him for being so considerate and putting himself last for the past eighteen years. In his logical mind, as a means of keeping his cellar doors shut, he simply wrote Anne's behaviour off as irrational and emotional nonsense. In his world, he was the dutiful man who had done the right thing for both his wife and family

This type of Blue behaviour is a good example of how the logical mind overrides all emotional considerations. When we say 'pull yourself together', we are really saying do not pay any attention to your feelings. Blue people will do almost anything to avoid facing their emotional boxes. They will prevaricate and sidestep, they will say 'yes dear' as a way of finishing or avoiding dealing with an emotional issue, anything to keep the door shut. The couple that have never had a cross word have managed this great feat by one of them going for a walk, or going to do the gardening. People who are unable to recall emotional confrontations in their relationships have kept their cellar doors well and truly shut.

Indigo sensitive locks

Indigo personalities have a great and useful grasp on both thinking and feeling. Their point of weakness is doing. Indigo people are sensitive. Very often they are sensitive in a way that means that they are unable to turn it off. This can be a very wearing place to be as there is no respite. These people are touched and concerned about the world, poverty and suffering because they can feel it keenly. The make up of their personality, compounded as it is by their inability to act, often leads them into avoiding difficult situations. The most common Indigo lock is isolation.

During the 1960s and 1970s, there were two types of people to be found on the road to India. The first were Yellow personalities who were involved in either avoiding commitment or seeking novelty, new experience and excitement. The second were indigo personalities who, having rejected the materialism (Greeness) and the violence (Redness) of western society, were searching for other answers in the east. Both Yellow and Indigo were able to communicate well as they had the thinking aspect of the personality in common. Yet there was something much deeper about the Indigos that the Yellows, try as they might, could not quite understand. When they got to the Ashram, both types sat to meditate, the Indigos lost in 'Ananda', a state of inner bliss, and the Yellows unable to settle, opening an eye from time to time just to check that they were not missing anything. Inside the ashram, there was no materialism and no violence.

After a while, the Yellow types became bored and wandered off to experiment with the local dope or to try another ashram. Sitting still and meditating was making the Yellows face inner emotional issues that they would rather not do. For them, acting, doing something else, was their applying their locks to their cellar doors. By moving on, they felt safe. The Indigos on the other hand were disturbed by the idea of leaving. They felt safe whilst inside the ashram. The violence and materialism that went on outside the wall could be forgotten once inside the ashram. In the ashram there was love, peace and happiness. Just as the Indigo avoided facing these difficult issues outside in the world, they also avoided facing these issues within themselves. This effectively means that Indigo types tend to use isolation as an avoidance that keeps the lock of their cellar door firmly in place.

Violet creative locks

Unlike all the other colours, Violet personalities exist in a relative state of balance. They are able to think, feel and do. It is this balance that allows them to manifest creatively. They have a clear cognitive image of what it is they need to do. They have an emotional commitment to it and they have the energy to make sure it happens. The option for this type of personality is whether they use this balance of qualities to create heaven or hell. We have all heard the phrase that genius is very close to madness. For the Violet personality, the issue is: will they use this gift of creativity to solve mankind's ills and beautify the environment, or will they descend into some lost and personal hell. Many artists draw out their blackest nightmares for all to see and many are tortured by negative thoughts and feelings.

Vincent was a quiet introspective child. He was born in Holland in March 1853. No one was sure what to do with him. Finally he worked as a clerk in an art gallery in The Hague, a job secured for him by his uncle. From here he was transferred to another gallery in London. It was here that he suffered his first period of depression after the failure of his first love affair. Depression was to remain a lifelong problem for him. During his search to discover a meaning to his life, he developed an interest in religion and later took a teaching post in England at Ramsgate. He eventually decided to study for the ministry, which, after a few years, he abandoned to become an artist.

Unhappy love affairs and depression seemed to dog his life and it is unlikely that he ever found real happiness. He met and developed a relationship with another artist, Paul Gauguin, who became a close friend. Together they attempted to set up an artistic community, which never worked. Their relationship became aggressive and violent and quarrelsome. During one of these arguments Vincent attacked Gauguin with a razor. It was after this attack, in a fit of remorse, that Vincent severed part of his ear. He was admitted to an asylum and suffered continued fits of depression. Later, after moving to a village near Paris, he began to paint his landscapes. It was here on July 27, 1890, that he shot himself in the chest with a revolver. He died two days later.

There are many successful violet types who do not kill themselves or slice their own ears off. The story of Van Gogh does illustrate just how close to madness many Violet personalities really are. For many, the motive force of their lives is their inspiration and their ability to create. Often it is this creativity that is the lock that avoids the need for them to look at the darker side of themselves. Often tied up somewhere in the inspiration is a figure who inspires the creativity. Both this figure and the creative process become the lock that keeps the madness in the cellar contained.

Magenta fantasy locks

Magenta is the opposite of violet. Violet creativity is an outward balance of the three areas of thinking, feeling and doing. Magenta is an internal balance in which the person has ceased to think, feel or do. Because of this, magenta is an internalised world that is the ultimate displacement activity, the ultimate lock. The purpose of the internal fantasy is to avoid whatever the external stimulus was that was beyond the person's ability to deal with or process. Most of these fantasies are warm and happy, though not all. Dreams can also come in the form of nightmares. By giving up the ability to think, feel or do, the individual produces the internalised fantasy over which they have no power. They have ceased to be able to control it and may be at the mercy of their own unconscious processes. If these processes are negative, the internal fantasy is like living in hell. I should say that most of the Magenta fantasies I have dealt with are warm cuddly ones.

A general note on people

If you have not yet read the previous books, I should just make a short addition to the locks listed above. You will probably have realised that all the personality archetypal areas described are to some extent within all of us. We all have all the drives, physical, social, intellectual, emotional, cognitive, intuitive, creative and fantasy within us. For a variety of reasons dealt with in the previous book 'What Colour Is Your Knicker Elastic?', we tend to focus on one or two of these drives that form the basis of our personality. You, as a unique individual, will be a subtle blend of the drives described above. You will find other people's blend of drive acceptable or repulsive, as described in book one, 'The Frog Snogger's Guide'.

Addictive behaviour

All personalities may at some time turn to addictive substances to keep their cupboard doors shut. All societies develop their own forms of anaesthetics that are essentially addictive, whether these are opiates, coca leaves, marijuana (now declassified to a class C drug), the heavier end of cocaine, crack and heroin, or our more normally preferred alcohol and nicotine. These are all locks in that they displace energy. But then so can hobbies, pastimes and beliefs. Anything that we do to displace the energy that we would be better off using to check out our cellar is a psychological lock.

When the lock fails

Most times when a lock fails, we will end up talking to a doctor. He will give us a diagnosis or label such as breakdown, depression, anxiety, panic, insomnia, obsessive compulsive disorder, post traumatic stress disorder, bereavement and so on. He may offer us a temporary lock using mediation such as Prozac or Seroxat. If we are lucky, he will refer us for counselling in the surgery, usually time-limited to around six sessions. If we are less lucky, we will be referred to a psychologist, with a current waiting list around three month to assessment and ten months to treatment. Failing that, it is out into the private sector to find a therapist that you will have to pay.

If you need a therapist, plug into your own network of friends and see if you can find one through personal recommendation. There are many accreditation systems that allegedly tell us that a therapist is worth seeing. This is sadly not true. To become accredited simply means that the therapist has filled out the right forms in the right way – it bears no relationship to their abilities as a therapist. Therapists, like builders, accountants and solicitors, are best found through personal recommendation.

9

Having Your Lid Lifted

Life begins at fifty

Of the three main reasons why the lids of unconscious boxes in attics or cellars are lifted, two are unconscious, but the third comes from an inner decision that we need to change.

> The first is the natural process of life and time normally seen as maturation, which happens below our awareness, that gently lifts a lid.
>
> The second is the traumatic removal of the lid following a difficult experience. This would be described as trauma or post-traumatic stress disorder PTSD.
>
> The third option is the province of those who are psychologically awake and aware enough to realise that change needs to take place and the levels of motivation to change are high.

When someone is aware and awake enough, they may well decide to lift a box lid to sort out the contents. When someone is doing this, it is what would be termed self-development of self-discovery. Most self-discovery starts with or is enacted through psychotherapy. While the majority of people seeking help through psychotherapy have arrived in the consulting room through the motivation of extreme mental, emotional or physical pain, there are those who arrive ahead of the pain.

The first type, which is the majority of people, have gradually been backed, or have allowed themselves to become backed, into a psychological corner. They are left with no alternative other than to find someone, anyone, who will help to stop them from hurting.

The second type are those who are aware that something will happen in the future and they want to deal with the issue before they get there. Being fully awake to what was happening, the GP with the brain tumour who knew it was terminal, initiated counselling sessions with, and for, his entire family to prepare them for the inevitable end, actually two years ahead of his death. It was the same for the manager who sought counselling ahead of her hysterectomy so that she would avoid the bereavement that she had seen in others.

Time for house work

However we get to the point, we will all at some time in our lives need to unpack or repack the boxes in the unconscious attic or cellar. This is a form of psychological housework. The housework in the attic is continuous, natural and ongoing. When we repack the boxes in the attic we are attending to our need to change our concepts of how we see, experience or perceive ourselves and the world around us. This is often the result of life experience and normally involves slow moderation through experience and time.

Can you remember what you were up to in adolescence? Embarrassing isn't it. If you are unable to look back at your youth and smile, laugh or even be a little, or a lot, embarrassed, the chances are that your concepts of self and the world have not changed very much. In short, you have not grown a lot. Those of us who become fixed in time, have frozen concepts. Normally we are stuck with fashion ideas or idioms of speech, 'man', 'babe', that pigeonhole us in time. If you are honest, you will probably find that you have something that has changed very little over many years. Maybe a saying, the way you walk or dance, an item of furniture or clothing. For me, it is desert boots. I have a pair on now, as it happens. I like desert boots. I tell myself that they are comfortable, and they are, but there is something about them that reminds me of something good. There is something about the good bit of the sixties that remains with me in the form of this footwear. What do you hang on to?

The timely house work of age

Changes in self-concept, or how I see myself, desert boots or not, may be age related or due to some personal development or even accepted rights of passage. For many, the ages of eighteen or twenty-one have significance of entry to adulthood. The ceremonies, parties and cards that attend these events imply that society, our family and our peers have granted new rights to us. In some way, we have come of age. The fact that others see us differently means that they will now treat us differently.

Those of us with user-friendly fathers may be taken down to the local watering hole to share our first legal pint. I have come across fathers who have paid an experienced and, I trust, healthy, lady of the night to initiate their sons into the wonders of the female form and the pleasures of the flesh. One oily rat that I knew when I was a teenager, had a wonderfully rich and generous daddy who gave him a chain of launderettes, across London, as his twenty-first-birthday present. The one thing that we can be sure of is that, once others perceive us and treat us differently, we will, as a consequence, also see ourselves differently.

There are other rights of passage that give us entry to certain social and psychological clubs each of which will require a change in the concepts held in the attic. These events may have unresolved components that we will also store in the cellar. The way in which we may be seen and treated differently may be because we have been found out or caught doing something that we should not. These may cause the change in perception to be negative so that we are shunned, avoided, made fun of, patronised or feared. Sometimes, negative accolades can give us status so that we may be seen as brave, cunning or hard. Or we develop the persona of the clever thief.

When I was a child at the time of the 'Great Train Robbery'

(1963), the general consensus that I heard from the adults around me was that had the chap, I think he was the train driver, not got hurt, then the gang would have been seen as heroes, not villains. The problem was that that driver might have been any one of them and that made the concept wrong. Taking from the rich and giving to the poor, the concept of the gentleman thief and the honour among thieves is all Robin Hood and Hollywood. When Ronnie Biggs was in his Brazilian hideaway, rather than being one who 'showed them what for' became someone who 'got away with it'. Not an easy concept in a society where getting away with it seems to happen to others and not us.

The fear of dying

In the consulting room, I regularly see clients who, beyond their presenting problem, are really scared of ageing. This is often related to the fear of dying and may have been set off by the death of someone close, perhaps a parent. The negative effects of death are often heightened when the person dying is younger. This is seen as fundamentally unfair. When someone dies after having completed their three score years and ten, there follows the concepts of fairness – 'well, he had a good innings, didn't he?' Or if someone has been terminally ill or in severe pain, there follows the concepts of rightness – 'well, it ended his suffering, didn't it?' Do you notice the question at the end of each of those statements? The question is important. It describes the fear and problems that the person has with their own concepts. They are seeking reassurance, in this case from me, that the person who died had it alright in the end, 'didn't he?' In another way, it is saying that I do not want to face the difficulties of a difficult death. In terms of attics and cellars, the ideal concept of death that I hold in an unconscious box in my attic, is a clean, peaceful ending.

> There I am, clean and tidy lying in bed. The family is sat around the room with warm and concerned expressions on their loving faces. I open my eyes and, as I speak, the entire room strains to hear my last words of wisdom. 'The horror that is an ending for a caterpillar is seen

> as the beauty of the butterfly in the master's eye', and with a knowing nod of the wise, I take a gentle last breath and close my eyes, letting go this mortal coil.

The problem is that my experience of the death of others leaves me with rather an uncomfortable box that is hidden in my cellar and contains all the qualms I have of how the ending will really be. It is this box that I avoid and this is the one that has all the energy of my unresolved fear.

> I am lying on a bed in a cold and clinical hospital room. I have tubes and wires connected all over the place and young nurses roughly engage in intimate activities that I wish they wouldn't. I am old, thin, yellow and disgusting. I have breath that would peel paint from doors I smell generally awful and am disgusted with my own incontinence. People are talking about me and over me as though I am not really there. I wish that the family were not there – that they could not see me like this – that they would just go away and let me die in peace. The pain is bad but I can't get my mouth to work to tell someone to turn up the morphine. I can hear the rattle in my throat and have all the fear of drowning.

None of us know how the experience of death will be presented to us unless of course we choose to write our own script and perform a well-orchestrated suicide. For many, the concept of death is something to be avoided. It often surprises me how often people distinguish between the state of death and the process of dying.

'It is not the actual dying I am scared of it is the process that will get me there that I fear'.

Dodging the concept of age

There is nothing more certain than the progression of the years. In a society where old age is generally seen as something negative, the concepts of looking young, acting young and being seen as younger than you actually are is important. The advertisers selling cosmetic surgery manipulate the concepts of the fear of age. We have only to see the evidence of the failed face-lift or the bad boob job to understand what lengths people will go to in an attempt to avoid the fears held in their cellar.

Our concepts of how we could or should look are not helped by the unbelievable images of Cher, or Joan Collins at the age of sixty-eight draped over her fifth husband aged thirty-six. For many, these images lead to a feeling that 'I', 'We' are in some way doing something wrong. Why do we not look like that? Is it money, is it face-lifts, do they really look that good when they take their clothes off? We can content our self with the idea that younger people only marry older people for money, but is that really it? Who is selling what concept to whom? It is what we keep in our attic that will wish Joan well with her good looks and her younger man. It is what we keep in the cellar that will be jealous and envious, 'He will leave her when he has had enough', 'when she is seventy-eight he will only be forty-five', 'she can't stay that good-looking forever'. Still we can all cheer up because it was on the news today, so it must be true, that 'they', the scientists, have discovered a new combination of supplements that are already available in health shops, that when used together, stop the ageing process and give us more energy and even restore our capacity to remember. Well, it works on rats, something about recharging the mitochondria in the cells. The strange thing is that, if it does work and we all take it, all we will do is move the concept of age up a few notches.

When the average age of death was thirty years, anyone who made thirty-five was extraordinary. Currently, the extraordinary people live to about one hundred and six years old and we have first-time mothers in their mid-forties and one rather odd lady, I thought, who had twins through artificial insemination at the age of sixty. I am told that for the coming generation, there will be people who will live to one hundred and twenty years of age. I suppose if they charge their mitochondria, they may make one hundred and thirty or forty. It may follow, especially with the development of hormone replacement preparations, that the concept of having children in our seventies will become commonplace.

The ones with noughts on

However we stretch the concept of age, the great marker in the conceptual cellar is the nought. Every time we hit a nought we undergo a strange metamorphosis. Why it is that being twenty-nine years and three hundred and sixty four days should be so different from being thirty years I do not know. Well I do, it is the concept – and that is actually the only thing that changes. We are no longer in our twenties, we have reached the dreaded thirties. The trouble is that the 'dreaded thirties' are followed by the 'dreaded forties' and the 'dreaded fifties' and so on. Attaining the age of thirty, forty, fifty or sixty will often involve a change in self-concept. The mid-life crisis, if such a thing actually exists, is assumed to be a response to the fears of ageing and being left behind or losing our personal powers. I have worked with many middle-aged men who have gone off with younger women and started families again, often as a way of showing themselves that they can. However we wrap it up, in terms of aging, it always seems to be the numbers with noughts on that have the greatest effect. The transition from being in your twenties to now being in your thirties can appear as such a great leap in time and age. The real leap is that from one conceptual box to another.

Life begins at fifty

Graham, a doctor and friend that I work with, tells of another doctor, a friend of his, who believes that the best years of life are the fifties. He sees this period, as a time when mortgages should now have been paid off, children, if not actually off your hands, are now diminishing responsibilities, it is the decade of freedom. He concludes that once you get to sixty, it is all downhill from then on, happy sod. I am fifty-one tomorrow and I have been sat here attempting to see this decade as the pinnacle of my life. Josh is now twenty-one months old and I am looking towards the ripe old age of seventy to achieve this free and wonderful decade of which he speaks.

There is some good news on the self-concept front however. Modern psychological research suggests that we are all getting younger. Not in the Peter Pan or the Merlin sense – of course each year we do all get one year older. This young-ness is in the nature of our attitudes and self-concept. It is estimated that we are currently ten to twelve years younger than the previous generation. This means that a person of fifty, me in fact, will have the self-concept and attitudes of someone of thirty-eight to forty a generation ago. My plan is that if we can keep the trend going in the same direction, by the time my body gets to being seventy years old my self-concept will be around fifty and the perfect decade will be mine after all. Mind you, in considering the people I do know, I think that twelve years younger may be a bit short of the mark. Some of the men I deal with act like they are ten-year olds when they are physically about thirty-five.

Back to lifting the lids

So as far as the attic is concerned, all experiences and rights of passage create the motive stimuli that lifts the lids of our boxes. In changing our concepts of ourself and the world, they change our perception. Equally, as our perceptions change, so does our experience – this is evolution at work. This will start at an early age with such ground-breaking experiences as weaning and potty training, and may go on to include transitions from schools, infant, primary, secondary, college and so on, to achievements in sports, tests and examinations, puberty, going abroad, flying, initial sexual encounters, jobs, marriages or secured permanent relationships, child birth, parenthood and so on. There will also be potentially negative experiences especially those of loss, divorce, death, and abandonment. Discovering that your partner is having an affair or is leaving you will have a profound effect on the way in which you see yourself. When we make bad judgements, get it wrong or get found out, we experience the negativity that will also change our self-concept. Such things will include all forms of disgrace and failure that lead us to become excluded from a group or organisation – being de-frocked, court-martialled, sent to Coventry, black-balled, demoted or simply sacked. Many of the latter will have repercussions for the material in the cellar which may cause the cellar doors to burst open, either because the cellar is full up and cannot accommodate anything else, or because there is some resonance with a past event or issues that we can no longer avoid, or simply that the lock that has been so effective up to this point no longer works.

Down in the depths

The need to sort out the boxes in the cellar comes about when we need to resolve some deeper repressed problem or issue. This often happens when our lock fails and unconscious material tumbles out of the cupboard as the doors burst open. Once the doors are open, we will, almost certainly, need some help and this usually means psychotherapy of some sort. The need to talk things through with another person is a basic human need. I do not however feel that counsellors, psychologists, social workers and so on, are the preferred option. Actually it is the other way round. Often the last person on earth you need to talk to is the professional. Sadly for many people the professional is the only option.

When we lived in extended families, we used grandparents, aunts, uncles, cousins and so on as a vital aspect of our natural stress-management network. When the Church was strong, and as a society we actually used it, we could talk things through with the priest or go to the confessional. When education was about people and developing the whole person, rather than creating automatons to improve statistics, teachers had time to listen. For some people, these roles have been taken on by social workers. For many, the bottom-line is that the only person available to talk with may be your local or workplace counsellor, psychotherapist or psychologist. It might be that or ring the Samaritans.

A common reason given for people having affairs is that they needed someone to talk to. Statistics suggest that 61% of people admit to having affairs and we have a nearly 50% divorce rate of those that choose to get married. A sad indictment of the way we live today. Perhaps you should all put this book down now and go and talk with your partners instead, or maybe you could read it together.

Why do we need professional help?

The short answer is that the majority of people really do not need professional help, if only they had some family to share their problems with. However, some issues do require more than a listening ear and may need you to be guided or enabled to face the unfaceable in that magic process of psychotherapy that allows the unconscious to become conscious.

If we are to enter the cellar we may need someone to hold our hand and or create a safe holding environment in which we can be honest with ourself and with another person. When I worked through my own cellar regarding my father and mother, I know that I could not have made that journey without the support and help of my own therapist. When we are facing deep, unresolved childhood issues, we become, for a time, that damaged child again. The child is the person who was unable to attend to the problems in the first place and had to consign them to the back of the unconscious cupboard to remain sane and safe. When we relive being a child, we are in a situation where the therapist becomes a temporary parent but not the bad parent that we experienced in the past. There is the transferential need for the therapist to create a safe holding environment and effectively become a good parent who will allow us to let the inner child come out to be accepted, healed or made whole. That may sound a little fanciful though this very process is enacted in many consulting rooms throughout the world every day.

Obviously, such relationships can be fraught with all the problems that transference can bring but, if the therapist is strong enough to support the client so that he or she can relive and resolve the past, therapy can be both swift and effective. Transference in therapy, the process whereby the client projects qualities, attitudes or feelings onto the therapist that do not belong to the therapist, will dissolve when the therapy is complete. At this point, the client will see the therapist more as they really are rather than an object fulfilling the transferential need.

Working in the dark

We will also need the skills of a professional psychotherapist when we know that there is something that is not quite right but we cannot find what it is, or it is in some way out of our reach. This is the Jungian concept of material that is inside us but beyond our control. In these cases, the cause of our problems is truly in the dark, the darkness of our unconscious cellar. The effect of this repression may manifest itself in many different forms. It might be anxiety, panic attacks or phobias and so on. Perhaps I am frightened of spiders. I know logically that I am several thousand times bigger than the spider and could squash it in an instant yet it fills me with terror. The phobia can be even more obscure. It might be pink bows, corduroy trousers or light bulbs. Whatever the cause, it is buried deep in the dark recesses of the cellar, so that all the cognitive thinking component of the issue is apparently lost, leaving me with the uneasy feelings of fear and anxiety.

Trying out temporary locks

The difference between the life-long locks of the previous chapter and temporary locks is that the temporary locks tend to be dangerous as they are often a short-term fix. Life-long locks involve a lifestyle that will go on for many years and may never be challenged or altered. The temporary lock is used in the short term if I am faced with a crisis that threatens to blow open the doors of my cellar. I experience the rush of klong and reach for the lock. There are three types of temporary lock that I can use to stop these things negatively affecting my everyday life. Ways of keeping it all inside under wraps so that I do not need to attend to it, so that I can pretend that it does not exist.

- The first is **medication**. This is often the product of a deal done with the regular pusher who is the GP. The GP sees the panic, sadness, fear or whatever and wants it to stop, wants you to feel better. The easiest route is to reach for the prescription pad. The result of this concept in the sixties and seventies was middle-aged women who had been stoned on tranquillisers for many years.

- The second are the **non-prescribed drugs**. These will include alcohol and nicotine but also the almost legal cannabis and all the other harder drugs that can be sniffed, snorted, injected or swallowed. All forms of medication when used as locks to make us feel better are really different forms of anaesthetic that we use to avoid looking in the cellar.

- The third is **specific displacement**. Displacement can be an ongoing lifestyle of general avoidance or generalised displacement. Specific displacement is when all the person's energy goes into avoiding the immediate problem that is right there and then in their face. The most common form of specific displacement is to attack – attack is the best form of defence, well, for some any way. You may accuse me of something or confront me with an issue that threatens to open boxes that I have skilfully kept closed. The fear of what might come out of the box is turned on you. Perhaps I will accuse you of something, perhaps I will shout and scream or in the extreme I might even attack you physically. All specific displacement behaviour is about keeping you away from my cellar doors. The bottom line is that I am scared.

The natural act of the conscious mind to repress difficult material in the unconscious mind is actually a loss of memory. Both permanent and temporary locks are only other forms of the natural lock that is repression itself. It seems strange to me that for beings with such a tremendous capacity to creatively solve problems, we so easily find ways to avoid them. We suffer from a general lack of honesty with both ourself and others. This is partly due to the culture of blame that surrounds us. If we dare to admit that we have got something wrong, we may never live it down. Forgiving societies, families, organisations, businesses and so on create a non-blame culture in which people no longer need to run for temporary locks as criticism ceases to be negative and becomes a positive gift of genuine feedback. Until we feel that we are in a situation that will allow us to share our deep inner self, there may be large areas of our unresolved past that will remain lost memories.

Dealing with lost memory

When circumstances in life lead us into a situation where we do need to face and begin to address our problems or negative feelings, we tend to look at our past experience as a way or means of understanding why we are like we are today. When undergoing therapy, the tendency is also to look backwards in an attempt to discover the cause of a problem. From this understanding we proceed to developing a resolution. It is here that we may hit the problem of lost memory. Our natural psychological anaesthetic of repression has been so good that all we are able to see regarding the issue at hand is nothing – total blackness. So people will say, 'I simply have no idea why I feel the way I do'. On occasions, the memory will be partly recalled and be fundamentally incomplete. 'I know there is a man standing in front of me. I can see his clothes and his hair, it's all shaggy and untidy, but I just can't see his face. Who is he?'

Sometimes the repressive process has been so efficient that whole areas of the past, many years, are only blank pages. People will report that they are unsure whether what they remember is actually their memories or something based on what other people have told them about event or family stories. This can also be true about images. Are the images real or things that have been processed from photographs? As a therapist, the one thing that I am sure of is that if the memory holds blank spaces the chances are that there are problems repressed there. The need to repress has been so great that whole periods of time have been lost. When I ask a client, 'what is your earliest memory?' and he or she responds, 'being ten years old', we need to discover why all that happened before that age has been repressed. Most bad or difficult things hide in the dark. When people have lost memory, they are hiding something that was too difficult for them to deal with at that time. To solve the problems in therapy, we must go into the dark unseen past. Often this is frightening but, as Susan Geoffers says in her book, 'Fell the fear and do it anyway'. There are times when there is no alternative.

False memory syndrome

So we dip into the darkness. Over time, we manage to get enough light in there so that we can begin to see. Seeing is the first part of understanding. Gradually, images are dragged up from the depths of the unconscious. Sometimes these are symbolic and may appear bizarre or disconnected. This is especially true of dreams that, during times of great psychological disturbance or therapy, can become Technicolor and arresting if not worrying. There will be times when the recalled memories will be immediately understood and represent the final pieces of a jigsaw that make the picture complete and allow complete understanding of a situation or event.

When discovering pictures in the dark, there is a common need to ask the question, 'are these memories real?' But do we know if what we remember is real? There has been much media copy concerning False Memory Syndrome. The first time I came across this, it was related to dentistry and certain forms of general anaesthetic used during dental procedures. Following the treatment, some women had experienced a form of sexual assault by the dentist. Now I am sure there are some dentists who would use the vulnerability of an unconscious and attractive women in their consulting room to satisfy their own needs, but we are not talking about that. What was happening was that, for some people, the anaesthetic had the effects of lifting a lid and either allowing something out or allowing something in. Let me explain. For most of us, going to the dentist is a scary and sometimes painful business. The heightened fear factor will make some of us opt for a full general anaesthetic rather than a local. We therefore know that these clients were in a state of heightened fear. We also know that pain and fear are two of the things that activate the mechanism of repression.

> **Allowing something out:** Let us assume that the patient was the subject of childhood abuse. The likelihood is that the abuser was male. It is also likely that the experience of being abused was both fearful and painful. Perhaps most importantly, the major factor in any form of abuse is the use or abuse of power as one person exercises power over another to meet his or her own ends. The person who is the victim of the abuse is essentially powerless. It is the powerlessness that creates victim-hood.

In this case, the similarity in the feelings between the original abuse and the dentistry creates a resonance that can bring apparently forgotten memories to the surface. We are powerless in the hands of a male figure that may cause us pain of which we are scared. The effect of the anaesthetic is to remove any locks that we might have used to keep the cupboard shut. For those of a Freudian bent, the fact that the dentist is male and is entering us through the orifice of the mouth may be an unconscious symbol of penetration. Many dentists have been wrongly accused of sexual impropriety under such conditions. I bet the dentists didn't bargain for that when they signed up for the job. In this situation, the memory may be more or less correct, it is just that the object and subject of the memory have become confused and attached to the dentist rather than the real perpetrator of the abuse.

> **Allowing something in:** Let us assume that the client was never actually sexually abused but is in some way at odds with a prominent figure from their past, perhaps a primary care giver who was a stepfather or a carer in a residential home. The actual real memory held by the client is that, after a fall in which she banged her chest, the

> care-giver picked her up, rubbed her chest and hugged her until she stopped crying and went off to play. In the replayed version, the memory becomes changed, mixed or distorted. The result is that the original act of kindness had been processed and rearranged. The recovered false memory is seeing the care-giver as rubbing her chest not as an act of caring but as an act of lust. The experience of pain becomes reprocessed into the result of an act of abuse.

I am not saying that abuse does not happen but there may be other interpretations of what we see as memories. It the case above, the likelihood is that the client had at some point experienced inappropriate erotic attention of some sort that we would label as abuse. The confusion of pain, fear and sexuality is being used to colour and reinterpret experience. These feelings become attached to the dentist as the available male figure.

We all suffer from false memory syndrome

It must be remembered that we all suffer from false memory syndrome. This is the essence of fantasy, not of what *will* happen but what *has* happened. When I replay events and scenes from my life, but re-write the script so that I said cleverer or more cutting things – that is the wonder of hindsight. The magenta fantasies that we have examined in the previous books are often the foundation of false memory.

Abuse and the images of abuse

Abuse, mental, emotional, physical or sexual, is much more common than we all admit. Around 80% of those people seeking psychotherapeutic help for any reason will report, when questioned, experiencing abuse as children. Most of that abusive material will be held in an inner unconscious box – a place of secrets that are seldom if ever told. The box may never be opened and the contents remain completely outside the person's awareness for their entire life. For others, the lid may be insecurely fastened so that the unconscious gradually seeps into the conscious. Or it may be that an incident or event rips the lid off so that, out of the blue, the person is required to deal with the raw reality and pain of the abuse as though it was happening there and then.

The emotions that explode out of boxes in this way are so real that they can feel as though they are happening there and then. This may include physical sensations so that the pain of early penetration may be experienced as though it is happening now. Many of the images that we recall of the abuse will be accurate and real. They may take time to appear clearly to the conscious mind but they will be true memories.

Sometimes, some of the memories will become mixed and distorted into false memories, so that when these stories begin to be retold, many will be factually false. That does not mean that abuse did not take place. What I am saying is that just as dreams comprise mixed and wonderful images that are of such a strange symbolic nature that they can lead us to wake in confusion thinking 'what on earth was that all about?' Yet these dreams have real and concrete content if we are able to decipher them. The unconscious mind is making connections and associations that may be true in a symbolic sense but untrue in a factual sense. If we experience in a very real sense that we have been, 'done to, abused, mistreated, shafted, screwed, crapped on', or whatever terms are appropriate, the unconscious mind may make some strange connections. In my own case, I relived a beating given to me by my father in several distorted forms at different times through my therapy. There were four distinct phases as the unconscious material was first recognised and then processed to a resolution.

First phase: dreams based in the real memory of my father beating me

Second phase: dreams based in the transfer of roles so that I was beating my father

Third phase: dreams based in me beating other people, including my own son, my mother, my wife and a boy from primary school who bullied me

Fourth phase: dreams based around me starting and stopping beating other people – making the decision not to do it.

It was only the first phase in the dream process that was actually real. The majority of stuff that my unconscious mind was churning out was the symbols of my progression through the problem. I have to acknowledge that the process was driven by psychotherapy that encouraged me to focus on my dreams as a means of monitoring my own progress. The journey as relayed in the symbols of the dreams is clear. It starts at the point of being a powerless victim and moves to a point of being able to exercise power. The key to the resolution is that once I had the power, I chose not to use it negatively. I did not develop the need to play pass the parcel and re-enact the negativity of my father. As in the game of 'pass the parcel', I unpacked the box and dealt with the contents. The abuse stops here. Well it does in my line of the family anyway. I do not know what my brother and sisters have chosen to do with their parcels.

Going it alone

I underwent my dream work within formalised psychotherapy. However, there are some things that can be done to either assist or avoid psychotherapy altogether. It is not obligatory to have psychotherapy to enable us to solve problems. People had and resolved problems long before the development of the psychological sciences over the last couple of hundred years. In the next chapter, I want to look at some ways that we open and examine our unconscious boxes and begin the process of dealing with the contents. These techniques can either assist or avoid the need for psychotherapy altogether.

Lifting corporate lids

The problem with the corporate persona is that it usually fails to include within it the Indigo aspects of deep sensitive insight into how it functions and the effects it has on those that work for it, live near it or around it, use its products or services or have to clean up the mess behind it. If the Indigo aspect of people was active in business, we would not have pollution or unfair practice. We would also see organisations that had the ability to be genuinely self-examining and able to put their own house in order. Thus the lifting of corporate lids would be a natural regulating process.

Corporate scandal

The alternative to having a natural regulating process is to have one imposed by a governing body or by the due process of law. Virtually all imposed regulation comes about when things go wrong. We need a death or disaster before organisations can find the will to get their house in order. The list is endless, Profumo, Bhopal, Aberfan, Bob Maxwell, Nick Leeson, Thalidomide, BSE, Enron, AIB etc. Individual therapy only works when both client and therapist engage with genuine honesty known as 'congruence'. Organisational well-being only comes about from corporate congruence, in short, when we are open and transparent and the things that we say we will do reflect what actually takes place. Hot in the news is the changing face of pension plans, where we can now expect thousands if not millions of people to be under-provided for in old age as distinct from what they were promised by the fund providers – this is incongruent.

10

The Housework in Your Head

Unpacking boxes

For most people, there will come a time when we need to unpack a box. I want to be a bit practical here. I started with my mother so I think we should revisit her in this last chapter. After my last book, *'What Colour Is Your Knicker Elastic'*, someone asked me how I felt about using my own material in the books, did I find that it was too self exposing or was I some sort of exhibitionist?

On reflection, I found that I had two answers to his question. The first is that for over my thirty years in practice, I have seen thousands of people for therapy. In each case, I have expected them to be open and honest with me about their closest held beliefs and secrets and their most intimate acts. It would seem rather dishonest of me if I did not apply the same criteria to myself.

The second is that I could present the things that I am trying to say as a set of theories. These theories would actually be no more than structural concepts held in my attic. By allowing you into my cellar we are examining reality concepts – this material is real. It is the reason that I became a therapist. Had my mother and father left me with noting to resolve, I probably would have become a banker or a doctor or something else that did not make any demands of me to open the cellar. Adding a foot note to this, I would say that I have learned more about myself in therapy as a client, and as a therapist working with clients, than I ever learned on a course. Courses impart structural concepts. We only truly know the theory when we have tested it into reality concepts.

So what do we do when we need to unpack a box? The need to do this is often our response to an experience that we have and we may be left with no choice other than to start unpacking. We are confronted by a percept that may be presented to us in a news broadcast, a newspaper, television soap, film, book or real life, that activates a concept held in one of our boxes. The response is completely spontaneously and unstoppable. We may be able to hold back the inevitable for a while with alcohol, drugs, religion and so on though in the end the energy will find its own way out. It is that something or event that has some deep resonance with our repressed material and jangles it up so that the lid flies off the box and the contents of the box tumble out. In my own case, it was the death of my mother that forced me to reopen and re-examine boxes in the dark.

My father as a lock

You will probably have gathered by now that my childhood was not that good – well, I didn't experience it as too much to get excited about. My father was a bully, an emotional pigmy who increased his own height by standing on other people, one of which was myself. We, the entire family, got the short end of his emotional immaturity from time to time, and even my mother took her fair share.

When I first went into therapy, my intention was to deal with my box labelled 'father', as he was the biggest burning issue in my conscious mind. I was as surprised as my therapist to discover that I was using my father as a lock to avoid facing issues about my mother. There was a very real box of unresolved emotional stuff relating to my father but I was using it in some way to avoid facing the material about my mother. Somewhere within my inner concepts I had developed a system that showed men as bad and women as good. I guess that it was a coping mechanism. Not only did my father beat me down but I was also the subject of bullying at school. I had no inner working model to allow me to see males in a positive light. My safe and secure times were when there was only my mother and my sisters there. The times when I felt able to just be myself were when we collectively did crafts, sewing, drawing and so on. I remember my mother unrolling some lining paper right across the living room floor so that we could all draw and paint together. As I watched in wonder, my mother crafted a Madonna and child with Indian ink. I thought she was so clever, I could only gaze in admiration – no, adoration. Women seemed so clever compared to men. At that time, all the women on the council estate did not work. Monday was wash day and Tuesday was ironing day and Wednesday we cleaned the house. Women seemed to live is this steady and constant rhythm. They seemed consistent.

The days – especially the summer days – seemed to pass in bliss until there was the sound of the key in the door. As soon as it became clear that my father was home, we all disappeared. Everyone would vanish to their bedrooms or find something that had suddenly become very, very pressing. As soon as he entered the house, the whole atmosphere changed. My concept was that males were bad and should be avoided at all costs.

Women were not like that. They were people to cluster around and greet warmly, not people to be avoided. Putting women in an exalted position made it easier for me to cope with my experience of men because I knew that when it came to it, women were safe. This led to an inner conflict in me in that, when I looked at myself as a male, I must also be bad. The structural concept that I developed to deal with this could never be confirmed into a reality concept – it was that there must be three sexes in the world men, women and me. I knew I was not a woman. I wondered for a time if I was gay. Though I have no prejudices against gay men, I have never met one that I fancied so I guess I am not. Finding myself to function quite happily in a heterosexual framework, I have settled for being a man who, they tell me, is in touch with his feminine side. As a child, I warmed to all the attributes seen at that time as being female – learning to knit, sew, clean, cook and so on. In avoiding all forms of masculinity, the negative feeling I had about my father acted as a lock that enabled me to avoid attending to my feelings about my mother.

My mother concept and my woman percept

My biggest piece of repressed emotion that emerged from my cellar relating to my mother was abandonment. She abandoned me to my father. She was not the woman who would stand between the child and the lion – she put the child between her and the lion. As an adult, I can understand her need for self-protection and survival. As a child, I felt very lost and alone. My mother helped to create the seed of my unconscious concept about what women are. This concept was the precursor of my unconscious percept. My structural concept was that women were good, soft, warm and supportive. My reality concept was exactly the opposite. Like everyone else, I played out my reality concept in my behaviour and this negative unconscious concept dictated the types of relationships and attachments that I made.

For many years, I spent my life making and breaking relationships with women and never understanding why this was, until I started to unpack the box and these things that were all unconscious gradually became visible. There is a lesson in this for all of us – the partner that we perceive to be ideal for us will, in someway be a reflection of the primary structural and reality concepts that will almost always come from our parents or initial primary caregivers. If I describe the kind of women I was attracted to before I unpacked the box, you will get a feel for the concept that I got from my mother.

In each case, (a) is what I experienced from my partners in the wooing phase and (b) was how I experienced it after it had developed.

Emotional warmth

(a) soft and warm emotionally, accepting understanding and giving
(b) hard, rejecting and critical

Enthusiasm

(a) open to new ideas and interested in my ideas at the outset
(b) self-opinionated, stubborn and fixed later

Selfishness

(a) prepared to take account of other's needs at the outset
(b) later egotistical and quick to take offence

Expressions of love

(a) admiring and complimentary at the outset, sexually loving

(b) moaning and critical later, sexually critical

Consistency

(a) caring and loving in general some days

(b) dismissive and abandoning other days

In therapy, working through the types of women I have been attracted to, I began to see that I was projecting my structural concept of my ideal partner onto women. It was only later, once the honeymoon period was at an end, that I could begin to see them as they really were, not as I wanted them to be.

As you have probably already thought it, I will deal with the issue of 'was it me?'. As in, was it me that was messing up the relationships so that there was a similar change in each person because I was the common factor? Through the process of therapy, I am comfortable with the idea that I was projecting, even hoping to see the characteristics of my structural concept in the women I chose. I was attempting to find a woman who would reflect my ideal image of my mother. What I was actually doing was picking out women who would repeat the same behaviour as my mother. They appeared to be caring at the outset but, when push came to shove, they were as abandoning as she was.

Preparing to open a box

I would like to say that I ended up in therapy because I was alert and awake and realise that I needed to change as a person. Actually, I ended up in therapy because I hurt. My relationships were bad and I felt that life was bad – I was definitely hurting. It is normally at this point, when are unable to deal with the pain any longer, that we seek some form of support or therapy. In most cases there is the overwhelming need to talk. It may be that we have good friends or an intact extended family that enables us to get things off our chests and in talking we begin to see a resolution.

The reason we seek to unpack a box is often unconscious – we just simply hurt. It is only once we are in therapy that we see the contents of the box, the source of our hurt. There are other occasions when we know that a lid is bound to fly. The event can become predictable, rather like those prone to epileptic fits who know that a fit is imminent and are able to get themselves to a point of safety. We may know that we cry at weddings, so we can predict that it will happen – that is the conscious bit. We may not know *why* we cry at weddings – that is the unconscious bit.

Some events build on each other in levels of magnitude. As one funeral follows another, the load of the emotion and grief is often accumulative. The emotion of the second reactivates the emotions of the first first, the third reactivates the first and second and so on. Sadly, funerals do tend to pile on top of one another as whole generations die in a short space of time. On the basis that the average length of time needed to grieve after a close loss is about two years, there needs to a be a reasonable gap between deaths to have any hope of avoiding the accumulation. Though, even if we think we have come to terms with a loss, we will never really know until it is put to the reality test. Whilst having all the advantages, support and kinship, extended families do lead to swaths of relatives departing close together. Commonly, the extended families of North Wales may lose ten close relative in an eight-year period. Some people never recover from such an experience.

My budgie has broken his leg

A box lid may be forced off, accidentally or vicariously, when we are not looking, as is well known by those working in emotive areas such as child abuse. On occasions, the box that is opened is not the one we were expecting. Someone may have attended for counselling for a completely separate issue to that which they end up working on. Perhaps their budgie has broken its leg and they have been deeply traumatised by the experience. It is only during the process of unpacking the box marked ‘Budgie’ that another obscurely related box resonates, pops its lid, and out tumbles a vast amount of material concerning Auntie Nellie and her death twenty years ago. This Auntie Nellie material is the stored emotional repressions that have never been dealt with and so Auntie Nellie becomes the focus of the counselling work. In this case, the counselling is the process that reveals the true cause of problem. The Budgie is a red herring and is avoidance, probably just one in a series of issues used to prevent the need to face the loss of poor old Nellie.

Avoiding the box

We do not however need a counsellor to tell us when a person is avoiding an issue. When a man has had a bad day at the office and returns home to kick the cat or shout at the kids, the problem has nothing to do with cats or kids – it is the office or, more correctly, it is the man's failure to deal with issues at the office that is the problem. The man's behaviour is an avoidance lock or displacement. Most displacement happens at an unconscious level – we just do it without thinking. Remember displacement is when we do something else to avoid any emotional or psychological discomfort, really a natural act of self-preservation. There are conscious forms of displacement that might have become enshrined into family tradition, so that if someone makes a noise passing wind in public, the response of 'more tea vicar?' or a shout of 'Taxi' serves to mask any embarrassment and avoids us facing that which we would rather not face.

Open the box

In the late fifties or early sixties, there was an awful quiz show called 'Take Your Pick'. Quiz master Michael Miles would ask contestants questions and, for each correct answer, he would increase a pile of money in front of them. On the back wall of the set were a series of lockers known as boxes. In the end, the successful contestant would win a key. They were then faced with a dilemma of whether to take the money or open the box. Inside the boxes were wondrous prizes like a holiday in the Costa del Sol. But there were also booby prizes like a baby's dummy.

As the hapless contestant struggled to come to a decision, the audience, encouraged by off-camera rebel-rousers, would be shouting 'take the money' or 'open the box'. Rather like our dilemma – do we take to avoidance or open the box and sort it out. For most people, when they approach an inner serious problem, there too are inner voices. There is the encouraging one saying: 'you can do it', 'go on, sort it out', 'you know you need to do it, so just get on with it'. The other, discouraging voice is saying: 'have another cup of tea', 'time is a good healer', 'better the Devil you know', 'you can't teach an old dog new tricks' and so on.

That internal battle can rage on and on. I see many people that know they should open a box and sort it out but somehow cannot find the willpower to do it. There are others who start to open a box and then wish they had not. So, before we go any further let me give you the official health warning.

When you open a box you do not know what you will find.
Once a box is open it may change your life forever.
Any changes in you will affect all those around you.

So on to opening boxes.

Opening a box in therapy

Most boxes are most effectively opened and dealt with in therapy. It may be that you have an idea of what the problem is and are able to go straight to the correct box. It may be that you have a feeling for something but are unable to find what it is, like something on the tip of your tongue that you are unable to remember. It may be that you are in therapy for one reason and another box flies open unexpectedly. If you do opt for therapy, here are some pointers that may help. I am using the word therapy in its widest sense and I am sure that many purists of counselling, psychology or psychotherapy will react against what I am about to say. I can only tell you that this is my experience – yours or theirs may be different. In terms of their ability to deal with boxes, I have given them a five tick rating.

Behavioural therapy ✓

As the name suggests, these forms of therapy are concerned with *what* you do, not *why* you do it. In terms of programming or conditioning, they are great but the ability to open and deal with boxes is very low – probably only worth half a tick really.

Bio-energetic therapy ✓

These are predominantly body work therapies and, at one end, involve touch therapies and acupuncture and at the other the soft martial arts such as Tai Chi and the yogas based around Hatha Yoga, Chi Kung and so on. While these are great for general self-development and for support while you are using other techniques to open boxes, as therapies they do not take us into boxes themselves.

Experiential therapy ✓✓

This is often group work. The energy of the group and the people of the groups are involved in individual and group development. These may include psychodrama and socio-drama, role-play, dream workshops, confrontation courses, anger management and even assertiveness, problem solving or support groups. Some groups may be focussed around the deeper work of opening boxes though the fact that it is a group setting and we are 'washing our linen in public', even if it is a select audience and can be inhibiting. Box lids can unconsciously fly off during these types of groups. Most group facilitators will have this covered, though you may be left on your own at the end of the group. When lids do fly, it normally takes other therapies to unpack the box successfully.

Gestalt therapy ✓✓✓

This may be either group or individual versions of the above and will generally be safer when working with a trained Gestalt therapist. Can be very powerful when used on a one-to-one basis and has some good techniques to get lids off and contents out. My experience is that the client needs to be fairly robust emotionally to benefit from Gestalt work.

Emotional therapies ✓✓✓

Much of what we store in our cellar boxes is emotion. It is the feelings of hurt, loss, grief, pain and so on that need to be released. It does not follow that the cognitions in the boxes need to be wedded to the emotions boxes for therapy to be effective. Let me explain.

Imagine that your unconscious emotions are held in a bucket and let us imagine that the emotion is in the form of water. From time to time, you add another cup of water until the bucket if pretty full. The water in the bucket has become mixed together so that if, at a later date, you dip in a cup to take some water out, you will not know where the water in the cup came from. It will be a mixture of all the cups of water you used to fill the bucket. It can be the same with emotions. They become mixed in the box so that when you let them out, you know you are venting feeling and know that it is doing you good because you feel better afterwards, although it might be that you do not know what it is you are feeling emotional about. Emotional venting therapies include catharsis, primal screaming, re-birthing, various forms of pranayama and various breathing techniques.

Rational emotive therapy ✓✓✓

This is a form of talking therapy that does try to take account of both cognition and emotion and as such can be a useful means of addressing the contents of boxes.

Cognitive behavioural therapy ✓✓

This is another talking therapy that for many people provides a quick fix. It is popular with GPs and some businesses because there is often immediate and sometimes dramatic results. The problem is that these apparent changes can be short lived. This statement is one that I have known to enrage my CBT colleagues. I have to say that I have worked with enough clients who have not benefited from the long-term effects of CBT to question it.

Analytical therapy ✓✓✓✓

This is a talking therapy with a difference. When it comes to getting inside boxes, analytical therapy is starting to get to the spot that counts. Analytically-based therapies focus on how what has happened in the past has an effect on the way we are now, and so see the reordering of the repressed material in boxes as the basis of therapy. The only drawback with this form of traditional analysis is the extended length of time that it takes and subsequently the amount of money it costs. Some forms of psychoanalysis require five one-hour sessions per week and this may last for between three to five years.

Hypno-analysis ✓✓✓✓✓

When it comes to dealing with boxes, hypno-analysis is the queen of therapies. The analytical part of the therapy reorders the contents of the box. The hypno part of the therapy removes the locks and barriers that keep doors shut and lids tightly on. This double-pronged approach makes this form of therapy very effective. The work that might be covered in five years at five days a week of traditional analysis can be collapsed into a much shorter time frame of perhaps one session per week for three months. The drawback here is that whereas counsellors are ten a penny, hypno-analysts are not so common. Good hypno-analysts are worth their weight in gold.

Person centred counselling ✓✓✓✓

This is a talking therapy that was initiated by Carl Rogers. It offers a very open approach that creates a space in which client can begin to address issues at their own pace. In such an environment, the natural tendency to open boxes is played out in a process that Rogers terms 'self actualisation'. This is an effective therapy though it is again prone to the long term as the course of the therapy is dictated by the client and therefore may prove costly.

Meditation ✓✓✓✓

There are many forms of mediation and some are more effective than others. Whatever the meditation technique, they all have the same goal and that is to still the mind by stopping the process of thinking. The inner stillness of meditation and contemplation can allow the same self-actualising process as person-centred therapy. As one eastern master described his counselling, 'he provided me with silence in which I began to hear the answer to my problems'. Meditation is effective but takes time to learn and to practice but then those that take the meditative path are usually making a statement about how they are living. The meditative path becomes a life-long one. Try my meditation course – The Knowing Silence – on the net.

Going it alone

We do not have to visit so-called professionals to enable us to open and resolve boxes. There are many techniques that can be used to address boxes and lift lids. The techniques described below can also be used within traditional therapy or alongside therapy.

Writing letters that are never sent

When the subject of a box is inaccessible – perhaps the person has died, moved away or is out of reach – we can begin to move material out of the box by writing it down. There is an important process here – when I simply *think* about things, they are merely reviewed and then put back in the box. When I *write* them or *speak* them, as in talking therapies, I have to process the information and organise it so that it makes good sense. Reviewed material remains unresolved. Processed material becomes resolved once it has been processed. Therapy journals and diaries are a good way of processing new memories.

Talking to the wall

Just as with writing, using a tape machine to talk to yourself requires processing. It also allows you to listen back, perhaps many times as the processes takes place. Taping sessions of traditional talking therapy can in many cases speed up processing and reinforces the work you have been doing in between sessions.

Spider-grams

If you have a more visual mind, drawing diagrams can be helpful so that a problem may be viewed pictorially. These diagrams have many names – in the sixties, they were called spider-grams, then became bubble diagrams. I have even heard them referred to, incorrectly, as Venn diagrams. Interestingly, Tony Buzan has hijacked them and now calls them mind-maps. Whatever the term, the process is the same. A spider-gram lays out the contents of a box and enables us to make connections between different issues and boxes. In the example below, the box label is 'Mother'. I am beginning to lay out the content of the box as I make connections. This diagram actually covered two sheets of A2 paper before I had finished.

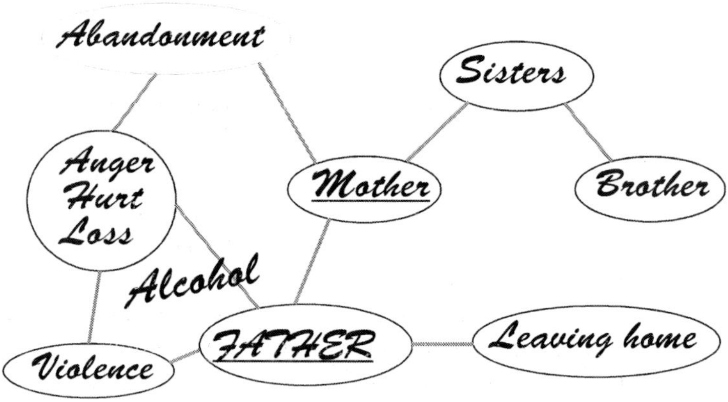

Each bubble (or box) in the diagram is actually the starting label for another diagram. Were I to continue with the same process, I would in the end have laid out all the concepts in both attic and cellar and made all the unconscious connections conscious.

Photographs and collage

Similar to a spider-gram is a visual collage using photographs, news cutting and various meaningful objects. A similar device is used with children when attempting to get them to play the box called family. This involves a box full of buttons that are laid so as to describe the family. In this case, size, colour and position are seen as important.

All these techniques are engaging the mind in processing. Some forms of art therapy using paints, clays and so on have similar effects. The immediate process of these techniques is working at an emotional level. It is in reviewing the results of the process after the exercise has finished that true understanding begins to dawn. Talking through the diagram, collage or artwork makes a cognitive connection to the feelings in the work.

The Life Box

This is a technique that I have used with many clients, most commonly those that were subject to childhood abuse. It can be used by anyone wishing to understand their life better. Beyond the therapeutic benefit of a life box, it is a fascinating record or archive, which in these day of genealogical research can be passed on to future generations.

It involves using a shoebox into which the client unfolds their life. Using standard 8x5 index cards and dividers, the box is laid out. Firstly the dividers are used to indicate the years starting with 0, then 1, 2, 3, 4 and so on. At the front of the 0 divider goes the birth card. This shows details of who you are and all that you know, have been told or can find out about your birth.

In the subsequent years, there are three kinds of card using different colours. There are cards that record basic cognitive material about what you can remember, cards that show how these things affected you at a feeling level and cards that show things that you have been told but do not remember. The cards may include spider-grams and collages, photographs or objects. Beyond the difficulties of dealing with cellars, the life box can be intriguing as a greater understanding of your life as it unfolds.

Filling in the gaps

One of the first things that becomes apparent is that there are areas, periods in life that are hazy, dim or completely blank. These are where the majority of your repressions are. Whatever the issues are, your conscious mind has committed them to the cellar and they are now out of your sight. In building your life box, it might be that you will need to use other techniques or go into therapy to shine some light into these darker spaces. Remember that analytical rule that when all that is unconscious becomes conscious, the therapy is complete.

Making connections

The second thing that we begin to realise is that we are able to make connections. If you have been completing your life box and discover that in year thirty you were being bullied by your manager there may a connection you can make with being bullied at school at the age of six. Similarly, those that have been the subject of continual failed relationships can begin to see connections and similarities. In understanding our problems, we can begin to understand the solutions.

The Life Cupboard

The issue of the life cupboard is the subject of future books that will enable us to understand the nuts and bolts of who we are and why we are who we are.

Cleaning out the cupboard

Whatever your chosen method, the result of cleaning out the cupboard is that you feel light, refreshed, relaxed, at peace and comfortable with whom you are. We all have a responsibility to do a little personal internal housework to ourself, those close to us, and the entire human race. It is only then that we can be sure that we are not an emotional or psychological pollutant that we are really free to live amongst others.

Keeping the cupboard clear

If we are to live in a peaceful inner environment and a peaceful world, we need to ensure that we keep our cupboard clear and do not continually harbour stores of repressed negative emotion. We all have a responsibility to clean out our cupboard, which probably means therapy of some sort, and to keep it clean usually means regular housework. Meditation, Tai Chi, one of the eight Yogas and so on all help us not to avoid issues. There are some basic principles that may also help that are as true for organisations as they are for individuals:

- **Act appropriately** (known as Dharmically in the east).
- **Help others and do not be selfish.**
- **Be honest in your thoughts, feelings and actions.**
- **Never leave what should be done undone.**
- **Do not bear grudges.**
- **Unpack your boxes when you need to.**

Most importantly:

- **Love yourself and love others.**

Time to wake up

Realising that you have an attic and a cellar and that your concepts are unique to you is an aspect of waking up. It is then that we can see other people as they truly are. The majority of people are actually deep asleep. Their level of consciousness is very low and, in the deep asleep state, assumptions can be made about other people and ourselves and our own limitations. Success and happiness are allied to waking up – it is only then that we can hope to reach our full potential. So I invite you to join me in the next book in this series *'Waking up is hard to do'*. It may be hard, but there are ways that we can do just that.

If you would like to contact me to discuss issues in this book or any of the others, please email me on **seanorford@aol.com**

Stay awake and be happy

Postscript

In the previous book, my email address was given as @cs.com. As Compuserve has now been taken over by AOL, it is now @aol.com. Please resend any lost emails.